ANTONIO BUERO VALLEJO

(the first fifteen years)

JOELYN RUPLE

ANTONIO BUERO VALLEJO

(the first fifteen years)

ELISEO TORRES & SONS
New York, N. Y. 10460

Ejemplar Nº)01597

© ELISEO TORRES 1971
P. O. Box 2
Eastchester, N. Y. 10709

DEPÓSITO LEGAL: V. 4.288 - 1971

IMPRESO EN ESPAÑA. PRINTED IN SPAIN, BY
ARTES GRÁFICAS SOLER, S. A., JÁVEA, 28, VALENCIA,
FOR ELISEO TORRES & SONS OF EASTCHESTER
AND NEW YORK, U.S.A.

1000149916

dedicated to Paul

ACKNOWLEDGMENTS

T H E research for this study was done at the University of Washington in Seattle. I would like to express my appreciation to the University not only for the use of the facilities, but also for the many benefits I have received off and on during the past twenty years. The people there who have been of help to me are too numerous to mention.

In addition I would like to express my appreciation to Antonio Buero Vallejo for permission to include the quotations from his writings, his patience in answering my numerous letters, and the time which he allowed me when he made his trip to the United States in 1966.

J R

BUERO AND THE SPANISH THEATER

BUERO THE MAN

A N T O N I O Buero Vallejo was born September 29, 1916, in Guadalajara. From 1934 until the beginning of the Spanish Civil War he studied sketching and painting in the *Escuela de Bellas Artes* in Madrid. The war years found him serving in the Medical Corp of the Army of the Republic. Following the war until February 17, 1946, he was held as a political prisoner. After his release from prison and until the premier of *Historia de una escalera,* his brushes provided him with a precarious living. Since 1949 he has been able to gain his livelihood by writing.

Deciding in 1946 to become a writer, Buero has through the years remained faithful to his dream of writing serious drama without compromising with popular or economic demands. His first published work was an extensive study on Gustave Doré in the ninth edition of *Viaje por España* by Baron Charles Davíllier. From the very beginning careful organization, loyalty to details, and a polished style have characterized his dramatic works.

Another landmark of his life occurred in 1959 when he married the actress Victoria Rodríguez by whom he has two sons, Carlos and Enrique.

11

In April, 1966, the Department of State of the United States brought Buero Vallejo to the United States for a two month visit of American colleges and universities as part of its cultural exchange program. At that time I met Buero personally and we discussed his work in detail. Prior to this meeting I had envisioned him as a composite principally of his characters Velázquez, Silvano from *Aventura en lo gris,* Silvero from *Hoy es fiesta,* and the painter Mauricio from *Madrugada.* In general he seemed much as I had imagined, and talked more freely about his work, literature, and conditions within his country than I had expected. He gave me evasive answers only when asked about his personal conflicts with his enemies and what might be unjust criticism of his work. He avoids speaking badly of others, and the moral factor appears stronger in his personal life than in his work. Also, in the past he had been so patient and considerate in answering my letters that I was surprised to learn that at times the demands of his public are a nuisance to him. Sometimes he would prefer to be left alone.

When I left my meeting with Buero I felt that I had been talking with a man who was, as Jean Paul Borel has suggested, truly the conscience of his era. At the same time I felt that the ideas contained in his plays were not always "finished" or "polished" ideas, but rather ideas in evolution, the germs of something that would be refined and translated into simpler terms for the masses by others to come later. For me his work represents the intellectual and spiritual explorations of one segment of humanity during an age of transition, and perhaps, an age of spiritual vacuum.

The Spanish Theater after the War

Buero's role in the rebirth of Spanish literature after the Civil War is of maximum importance. Immediately after the war most Spanish intellectuals were in prison or left the country in exile while the Second World War hampered the nation's economic recovery. As far as literature was concerned, immediately after the war some love themes appeared in the poetry, but these disappeared quickly under the hard reign of Franco. José Narcisidor in 1952 described the common denominator in literature at that time as "pessimism, bitterness, fatality, defeat." [1] Although this is true, it should also be noted that this literature only expressed the frustrations of the time, and in so doing represented the rebirth of Spanish culture after the war. The characteristics may be negative in that they reveal the unhappiness and the suffering of the people, but they are at the same time positive in that they indicate the beginning of a new, more positive attitude.

During the years immediately following the war the government used the theater and movies for propaganda. There were translations of works from other countries, presentations of the Spanish classics, and some works by contemporary writers, but works censored and in general of limited value. [2] This period also represents the gestation of the theater of escape which Enrique Llovet has

---

[1] "La literatura española bajo el signo de Franco," *Cuadernos Americanos,* iii (1952), 26.

[2] Medardo Fraile, "Twenty Years of Theater in Spain," tr. Mildred Boyer, *The Texas Quarterly: Image of Spain,* 1961, p. 97.

described as "a unilateral theater, a little timid, that never ceases to arouse passions, that uses fantasy instead of emotion, which lacks sincerity and valor, which is separated from the two great popular themes, but which is theater, well done and well written, has sensitivity, and is outlined with the greatest dignity. This theater opened its doors the 29th of April, 1949, the night of the premier of *Alberto* by José López Rubio." [3]

Also from a positive point of view, Spain had more small theaters than ever before in her history. The government maintained two official theaters, the *Teatro de María Guerrero* and the *Teatro Español,* and began to offer awards in order to stimulate theatrical production. Students became interested in the theater as a means of expression and fought to protect it from the bureaucracy. Although the number of outstanding serious authors since the war has been small with all the critics in agreement only about the importance of Buero, some younger writers such as Sastre, Olmo, Muñiz, Martín Recuerda, Mañas, Rodríguez Buded, and Gala promise much for the future.

BUERO'S INFLUENCE IN THE SPANISH THEATER

Buero entered the dramatic scene in 1949. That year the city government of Madrid decided after a fifteen year suspension to begin awarding the *Premio Lope de Vega,* part of which consisted of presentation of the winning work in the *Teatro Español.* Antonio Buero Vallejo,

---

[3] *Don Juan y el teatro en España,* ed. Juan Gyenes (Madrid, 1957), p. xix.

an unknown, won the prize. Although he has since then been awarded additional prizes, this is the only competition that he has ever entered. The premier took place only a few days before the annual presentation of the *Tenorio* by Zorrilla, but the success of *Historia de una escalera,* the winning work, was so unexpected and complete that they suspended the *Tenorio* for the first time in the history of the theater and continued with *Historia.* Today this play is almost a classic. It was the first theatrical work presented in postwar Spain which showed signs of great originality and talent. Since then Buero has come to be generally accepted by the critics as Spain's leading serious playwright.

During recent years his influence has been obvious in the dramatic work of contemporary writers. Some critics in Spain have commented upon this influence in Olmo and Muñiz, in the latter particularly during his early work. They have also suggested that *Las Meninas* could be a predecessor of *El caballero de las espuelas de oro,* a play about Quevedo by Casona, and made comparisons between *Un soñador para un pueblo* and *Epitafio para un soñador* by Adolfo Prego. In addition, critics have at times complained of having seen far too many imitations of *Historia* and said that they would like something a little gayer.

The influence of an author in other authors is a subject requiring more careful, detailed analysis than is undertaken here, but still some similarities of form and subject matter seem too flagrant to debate. For example, *El baile* (1952) by Edgar Neville follows the precise, careful construction of *Historia* (1949), but in a lighter vein. In the first act of *El baile,* taking place in 1900, Adela lives happily with her husband and his friend. In the second act, twenty-five years later, she has grown older, and in the last act she has died and the husband and friend are reliving the past through the granddaughter. In *Historia* ten and twenty years pass between acts and the emphasis is also on the changing generations.

La madriguera (1960) by Rodríguez Buded resembles *Historia* but in a different way. It depicts the lives of several people living in a rooming house chained to their circumstances as the characters in *Historia* were chained to the stairway. Different occupants in the rooms indicate the passage of time.

Alfonso Paso at times has situations similar to those of Buero. In *Los pobrecitos* (1957) Leonor steals money and deceives the poor in order to give it to them and help them. The poor accept the money as a miracle sent by God. In *La señal que se espera* (1952) Susana plays a harp deceiving the others and letting them believe that the harp played by itself—a miracle. And there are other examples.

Buero's influence appears less obvious in the form of works of social protest written during the past few years with relaxation of censorship, such as *El grillo* and *El tintero* by Carlos Muñiz, *La camisa* by Lauro Olmo, and *Las salvajes in Puente San Gil* by Martín Recuerda. But although these writers show signs of definite originality, their works follow Buero's path in that he was the first of the postwar writers to abandon the evasionistic line and attempt serious expression of contemporary problems.

Today the future of the Spanish theater depends upon the work of Buero and these younger writers. In writing about the theater in December, 1963, Enrique Llovet said,

"The number of writers among us is very limited. With the exception of Buero Vallejo, the others—except for some of the young ones—belong absolutely to the evasionistic line... They have turned their backs to reality." [4]

This does not mean that Buero has always produced masterpieces and had great successes. Actually, some of his plays have been flops before the public. *Casi un cuento de hadas, La señal que se espera,* and *Irene, o el tesoro* were not at all well received. [5]

In addition Buero has had problems with the censors, as has probably almost every Spanish playwright. He wrote *Aventura en lo gris* in 1949 but could not get it approved. In 1963 an opportunity arose to present it. Bad reviews killed a successful first night. Since the government controls the press, it may have been indirectly somewhat responsible, but that cannot be proved. The political situation at the time suggests that possibility. Local authorities have forbidden presentation of *Un soñador para un pueblo* in two cities, but it is permitted in other parts of Spain. *Las Meninas* ran in the *Teatro Español* from December, 1960, until April, 1961, and was scheduled to finish the season. It was still playing to full houses when the government decided to cancel the production in order to celebrate the fiftieth anniversary of *En Flandes se ha puesto el sol* by Marquina. This is a little hard to understand because the fiftieth anniversary was in 1960, and the celebration in the spring of 1961. During the season of 1964-65 Buero could not present his new play *La doble historia del Doctor Valmy* for reasons which are not

4 *Insula*, no. 205, 4.
5 Fraile, op. cit., p. 98.

clear. This play has since been published in the United
States in the bi-lingual magazine *Artes Hispánicas* (published by Macmillan Company for Indiana University,
Autumn 1967, vol. 1, no. 2.) In the fall of 1963 the
government forbad the presentation of Buero's works in
the two national theaters because he had signed a petition
in favor of the Asturian miners. [6] As if this were not
enough, at times when he has presented controversial works
such as *Un soñador para un pueblo* and *Las Meninas,*
some of his friends have failed to defend them.

The true full story of his troubles with the censors
and others of like mentality will probably never be known,
for they often use indirect methods to achieve their ends,
such as unexplained cancelling of contracts, anonymous
threatening phone calls, public defamation by radio and
television, and verbal rather than written threats. What
records there are are not open to public inspection. And
furthermore, Buero seems extremely reluctant to talk about
this aspect of his work.

LITERARY INFLUENCES FOUND IN BUERO'S WORK

Although Buero's work has an international appeal, he
is essentially a Spanish writer reflecting the liberal, pro-

---

[6] This is as it was reported in *Hispanic American Report*
(xvi, 10, Stanford University, Dec. 1963, 13). I have been
unable to obtain further information regarding their source of
information. Such prohibition was never expressed directly to
the author. Buero has affirmed that he signed the petition fully
aware of the consequences that might follow. Regardless of what
took place, the fact remains that he did not present anything in
the national theaters during the years immediately following this
incident.

gressive development of his culture. In such social works as *En la ardiente oscuridad, Hoy es fiesta, Madrugada, Las cartas boca abajo,* etc., one can perhaps see some influence of such American writers as O'Neil and Wilder, but for me they reflect little more than the natural development of the Spanish theater, a more critical examination of a social theater previously rather timidly explored by Benavente and prior to him, by Moratín.

Jean Paul Borel describes this evolution very well in his article "Teatro de lo imposible," [7] in which he envisions Buero's theater as another step in the development of the twentieth century drama which began with Benavente. Benavente portrayed a society content to live with its blindness, to cultivate the lie, the error, the compromise. Later Lorca proclaimed the value of love and its impossibility with human sensibility shaking upon its very foundations. Unamuno represents a step between Lorca and Benavente. For him intellectual and spiritual life does not find in modern society the conditions necessary for its development. Unamuno feels our humanistic culture has ended because it has lost its sensibility to the human aspect and "left man reduced to a role by which he serves ends which escape him." For Borel the step preceding Buero is Valle-Inclán, who conceives the greatness of man in his rebellion toward the limitations placed upon him. In Buero one finds a synthesis of these four writers plus the addition of an analysis of society which avails itself of modern psychology and sociology.

In addition to what Borel has stated, I would add that Buero goes deeper than the others, with perhaps the

---

[7] *Insula,* Oct., 1961, p. 15.

exception of Unamuno, in his probing of the transcendental. Also, Buero excels Unamuno in that while Unamuno had many things to say, he had not mastered the
dramatic technique. Buero not only has something to say,
he knows how to say it.

One can easily see many other influences of Spanish
literature in Buero's work. Like all Spaniards, he possesses
his own particular brand of "quijotismo" which comes out
in a great variety of rebellious dreamers. Calderon's "life
is a dream" theme, which will be discussed in detail later,
frequently appears. Buero considers Galdós as one of the
major influences in his work, particularly in the treatment
of religious matters. Like Galdós, Buero is essentially a
religious writer in spite of the fact that he does not treat
the subject directly. The clergy which he includes create
an atmosphere, often of aloofness, which by its very nature
carries the connotation of hypocrisy. Like Galdós, Buero
questions where one finds virtue, and concludes, like Galdós, that it is not always where it should be.

As far as foreign influences in Buero's writing are
concerned, I do not think they are significant, although
Buero is well read and familiar with the work of other
important literary figures of this century. During the
Spanish Civil War and the immediate postwar period
Spain was almost completely isolated from the rest of the
world, and she herself was devastated. While Buero might
have had the opportunity to read some books during the
war and while in prison, it seems extremely unlikely to me
that the library was extensive.

Because of the didactic tone, although Buero has repeatedly asserted that his work is not didactic, one may
be tempted to try to relate Buero's work to that of Brecht.

Buero himself has said that he considers Brecht's influence practically nil. Remembering that the formative period of Buero's literary career occurred during the war years when Brecht was an exile from Nazi Germany, it seems unlikely that his works would have been available in Spain. Of course the possibility remains that he may have read Brecht during his adolescent years. That Brecht is not too well known in Spain is further borne out by the fact that it has not appeared on the Spanish stage. Buero's adaptation of *Mutter Courage und ihre Kinder* in the autumn of 1966 will be the first commercial Spanish production of a Brecht work since the war years. [8]

In addition to these factors, a strong Brecht influence seems unlikely because the two men have very contrary philosophies as to the role of the theater. Brecht favors a committed theater, and Buero feels that the more hidden the author's opinion, the better. For Buero, if a play is a true work of art, two people with completely opposing points of view can observe the play and enjoy it. The theater is not a didactic vehicle, although he recognizes its political influence, but rather an art form exposing the different facets of the problems presented. And in spite of Buero's interest in the welfare of his nation, his compassion for the poor, and the moral tone of his work, he is over and above all an artist.

---

[8] It ran from October, 1966, through January, 1967, in the theater *Bellas Artes* in Madrid and marked Buero's return to the theatrical scene after the previously mentioned difficulty with the authorities in 1963.

CLASSIFICATION OF PLAYS

I N order to provide the reader with an idea of the different types of plays which Buero has written, they are classified here as experimental, social, and historical works. This classification includes everything published to date with the exception of *Hamlet, Príncipe de Dinamarca,* a translation of the work by Shakespeare.

Buero believes the theater needs new blood, and for this reason from time to time he has written "experimental" plays. In one sense every play is an "experiment" — sometimes successful and sometimes not. In another sense, a change of form makes a work truly "experimental," for form is the only element in literature the writer can change. If he tries a form which varies from the current style, the spectator or reader usually notices. At times a form new to the author does not seem new to the reader, or the author may handle it so well that the reader or spectator fails to notice it. As a result, what may be experimental for the author may not necessarily seem that way to the reader or spectator, and what seems experimental to one person may not appear that way to another.

En la ardiente oscuridad illustrates this. Buero has described the play as perhaps the most experimental of all, but because of the powerful tragic effect, probably few viewers would think of it in that way. The plot revolves around a blind boy's search for "light," the symbol of transcendental truth.

Casi un cuento de hadas seems more obviously experimental. It is an adaption of a children's story by Perrault. Leticia, the stupid beautiful princess, lives in the palace with her parents and ugly sister and plays with her dolls. Her prince charming, Riquet, as ugly as she is beautiful, comes to court her. During the course of the play he makes her intelligent and she makes him beautiful. The play is a fascinating study about personality presented in a somewhat unfamiliar manner.

La tejedora de sueños is another experimental work, an adaptation of a theme from Homer's *Odessey*. Penélope weaves during the day and unravels her work during the night while she awaits Ulysses' return from the war — a very human story of the women who wait at home while their husbands are away at war, a situation as common now as during the time of the Greeks, with an experimental presentation.

Irene, o el tesoro raises the ancient question of reality. Everybody believes Irene is crazy and mistreats her. In the end she commits the only suicide in Buero's dramatic work. The censors almost always prohibit suicide in the Spanish theater. They probably permitted it in this case only because Irene was crazy, or "enlightened."

Aventura en lo gris, another experimental work, again searches for the meaning of reality. The action takes place at the border of the imaginary country of Surelia. During the first act, taking place in the evening, refugees arrive fleeing from the war. A dream interlude follows this act, and the second act takes place the following morning.

In addition to these arbitrarily classified experimental plays, we find many other experimental elements in Buero's theater, such as the setting of a play on a very undramatic, old tumble-down stairway in *Historia de una escalera,* the use of music to express the inexpressible in *La tejedora de sueños, La señal que se espera,* and *El concierto de San Ovidio,* the suggestion that love is not what it seems to be in *Madrugada,* the use of such unlikely themes as the meaning of miracles in the 20th century in *La señal que se espera,* and the constant attempts to reverse the situation and view it from the other side.

Leaving to one side the experimental aspect, Buero has written social plays which reveal the customs and characteristics of Spanish life, such as *Historia de una escalera, Hoy es fiesta,* and *Las cartas boca abajo,* which take place in Madrid, and *El terror inmóvil* which is placed in one of the provinces. These plays concern some incident of contemporary life and reveal the drama latent in the ordinary. As a rule these plays lack spectacular events. Although Buero has commented that he did not intend *La señal que se espera* and *En la ardiente oscuridad* to be this type of work, nevertheless to some readers and spectators they may seem more social than experimental.

Madrugada could also be classified as social or experimental, depending upon the point of view.

Las palabras en la arena, a short one-act play based on the story of Jesus and the adultress, probably would also be best classified within this group, for like the others it depicts a hyprocritical society in a very simple, realistic manner.

The third group, the historical trilogy, includes *El concierto de San Ovidio, Un soñador para un pueblo,* and *Las Meninas.* These plays contain a majesty not found in the others. They take the viewer to another world, but a world nevertheless containing the problems of contemporary life. The dramatic technique in these plays differs markedly from that used in the others in that the scenes change frequently to comply with the much more active plot. The plays do more than talk as time marches on. *Concierto* contains only ficticious characters with the exception of one while *Soñador* and *Las Meninas* draw heavily upon history for the members of the cast. Although Buero Vallejo maintains he is no research expert, careful analysis of the historical aspect of his work indicates an exceptional understanding and interpretation of history. When he embellishes something, he does so for dramatic emphasis or to clarify his point, which in effect are the same thing. These historical plays search the past in an attempt to understand and explain the present.

This study will consider in detail all Buero's plays with the exception of two: *Hamlet, Príncipe de Dinamarca* and *El terror inmóvil.* Buero is not a translator and he is not happy with his translation of Shakespeare. He did it because he was commissioned to do so. It bears no relation to his other dramatic work. *El terror inmóvil,* one of his first plays, was never presented before the public. The second act was published in the anthology *Número 100* in 1950. The plot deals with a domestic situation in which the overly severe father forbids the family to take photographs of the eight year old son. An uncle takes a photograph and the father destroys it. The elements which merit attention are developed with greater clarity in other works.

POLITICAL ASPECT

J E A N Paul Borel has said that for Buero politics and the theater are two parts of the same thing.[1] If one defines politics in the broad sense of the word, perhaps we could agree. Buero himself has repeatedly affirmed both publicly and in his work that a writer has a moral obligation to concern himself with the political welfare of his nation. Many of the ills to which his literary creations fall subject result from their negligence or indifference to their responsibilities in helping shape the destiny of their culture.

In spite of this, Buero has been criticized by fellow countrymen for not taking a more active stand against the lack of civil liberties within Spain. For example, Alvarez in discussing *Las Meninas* in the magazine *Indice* maintains that Buero exploited the figure of Velázquez and the historical atmosphere in order to express his own ideas, but in so doing said nothing new. According to him, any one of the editorials in the magazine *Indice* affirms more than Buero.[2]

---

[1] "Buero Vallejo: Teatro y Política," *Revista de Occidente* (Madrid, August, 1964), 226-234.
[2] "Un Velázquez de ocasión," XII, 145, 27.

While an American cannot very well evaluate how well
Buero fulfills or fails to fulfill his civic responsibilities, it
seems to me that he is extremely well informed about the
domestic situation in Spain. He possesses a reflective
personality, and like most men who are able to envision
the numerous facets to the problems presented, reacts more
slowly than the more passionate individual who can incite
the masses to riot. However, history seems to indicate that
while a reflective personality may never get around to do
anything sensational, in the long run his ideas stimulate
the action. Whether this is true of Buero or not, only time
can tell.

In commenting upon the influence of the theater
within a culture, Buero has stated that he conceives this
influence as being of a collective political rather than of
an individual social nature. At the same time he recognizes
that a committed theater could be dangerous. The theater
as a political influence within a nation must be used with
discretion. Visualizing the effects of his work in this way,
he sees no reason to attempt the politically impossible, but
rather contemplates the possible results of his efforts with
the same cool equilibrium which he displays in creating
his dramatic situations.

The groundwork for Buero's dramatic career was laid
in prison. Immediately after the Civil War about half the
nation was either in exile or in jail. Convents, seminaries,
bull rings, warehouses, any building with bars on the
windows served as a jail. Men were sentenced by military
tribunals as being guilty of rebellion or support of rebellion
according to military code, often without proof. All officers
were automatically jailed. But those who were only imprisoned were in one sense lucky, for many others were

shot. Political prisoners were mixed in with hardened
criminals, and the country was told there were no political
prisoners until many believed it.

Manuel Amblard in his article "23 Years in Franco's
Jails" [3] has described life in these prisons. According to
him, at the beginning the Jesuits and Dominicans disputed
the chaplaincy of the prisoners. All except the Moors,
including Protestants and Jews, were forced to attend
religious services. Anyone baptized a Catholic was considered a Catholic and expected to behave as such. As late as
1961 prisoners were punished for refusing to attend Mass.
During the first years of Franco's reign Mass was a political
act. Many prisons used the Falangist flag as an altar cloth,
and the celebrant at the end of the Mass raised his hand in
the Fascist salute. Sermons often consisted of insults and
curses. Although confession and communion were not oblig-
atory, political pressures made them hard to resist. Com-
mutation of sentence was promised to those who took
communion, but these promises were not kept. In considering these remarks by Amblard, it must be remembered
that during this period emotions were extremely tense.

Care of the prisoners was unbelievably bad. The dying
were at times kept in isolation and denied medical care.
The official physician at the prison at Burgos immediately
after the war was so incompetent that the Medical Society
of that city forbad him to operate, according to Amblard.
Many prisoners died of hunger while the nuns stole the
rations in the kitchen. After a while the General Admin-
istration of Prisons replaced nuns with civil servants, supposedly because of their inefficiency.

---

[3] *The Nation*, 200, 12 (March 22, 1965), 305-307.

Amblard has stated that 90 % of those released from prison after long captivity suffered from incurable digestive tract ailments. It would be interesting to know how he, a prisoner, was able to arrive at this figure, and in deploring these conditions we must keep in mind that people were starving outside of prison also.

The incidence of mental illness among the prisoners was high. After five years all suffered prison psychosis. Terror replaced discipline.

Books and magazines were censored by the chaplains with Ortega y Gasset, some of Galdós, Valera, and Unamuno banned. Study of English was practically a criminal offense. Amblard mentions that some prisoners painted. Buero sketched many portraits during his prison stay but did not work with oils. In order to obtain oils he would have had to compromise himself with the authorities — something he refused to do. On his record "Me llamo Antonio Buero Vallejo" he mentions his lack of opportunity to paint during the ten years of the war and postwar period.

With time conditions within the prisons improved. Various groups throughout the world continued protesting treatment of political prisoners even up into the 1960's. Also, younger, less embittered men began to replace the older guards. These younger men were often surprised to find they were guarding men as well or better educated than themselves and no more dangerous.

Leaving prison presented other problems. Often the prisoner returned to a society which had more or less forgotten he existed. Housing was scarce with food and work scarcer. In addition, the prisoner had forgotten how to live and act away from the rigidly supervised prison life. Liberty offered numerous adjustment problems.

It seems to me we can see references to this prison life throughout Buero's work. Like the prison nuns the prioress in *Concierto* steals food from the blind inmates of her institution. The theme of fear and loss of personality as the result of oppression, either physical as in *Concierto*, or economic as in *Historia*, reoccurs again and again. Buero portrays numerous individuals with handicaps, both physical and emotional individuals whose minds and bodies have been unable to adjust to the limitations of the environment. All his work cries out for freedom of expression, freedom from restrictions imposed by an outside human force. And morality — each play he writes begs man to improve himself and to cease inflicting his cruelties upon his fellow men.

Continuing to more specific observations about the relationship of Buero's work to the political situation, his first plays, all written before the end of 1947, were *En la ardiente oscuridad, Aventura en lo gris,* and *Historia de una escalera,* probably written in that order. In the first, *Ardiente,* we find a philosophical or religious struggle within the protagonist as he pleads to society to look about and see the conditions under which it actually exists, to stop pretending that all is right with the world. Although Buero probably made some rather fundamental revisions in revising the edition of *Aventura* now available, he still protests a lethargic society which refuses to recognize and reject a dictator. *Historia* also points out the abulia of a society which talks about escaping from present circumstances but does nothing more. To a young man who had just spent seven years in prison, the moral indifference of the outside world must have been extremely depressing.

Certain events within Spain during these first postwar years also probably influenced Buero's attitude. [4] Going back in history a bit, in 1941 a new "modus vivendi" temporarily replaced the Concordat of 1851 with Rome which had been invalidated by the Constitution of the Spanish Republic. This "modus vivendi" provided that the Catholic Church be officially recognized by the government, that education in lay schools conform with the Catholic religion, and that the bishops and clergy look after the spiritual life of the nation's youth with no state interference. In 1953 a new Concordat replaced this "modus vivendi." One can perhaps see the spirit of the "modus vivendi" expressed in these first plays in the inflexible *moral de acero* of the school for the blind in *Ardiente* and in the pretty words which Carlos in *Aventura* needed in order to give his life meaning. In both cases spiritual strength comes from an artificial outside force rather than from within the individual.

These first postwar years found Spain pretty much cut off from the rest of the world. During World War II a volunteer group of Spanish soldiers served on the Eastern Front with the Germans against the Russians, and after the war ended many Western nations saw in Spain remnants of the Nazi movement. In 1946 the General Assembly of the United Nations imposed a diplomatic ban against Spain. While other European nations received

---

[4] Unless otherwise indicated, the following historical observations are based upon the information published in *Hispanic American Report* by Stanford University. I recognize this source at times contains quite serious errors, but nevertheless feel it probably presents as unbaised a reporting as is currently available.

Marshal Plan Aid to help their economic recovery, Spain did not receive any until 1952. In order to counteract this negative world opinion, Franco began to play down the importance of the Falangists, which reminded many people of the brown shirts, and began to exploit his condemnation of the communistic menace. In the long run it was this exploitation of the dangers of communism which gained him recognition by the Western world.

Because of this economic isolation Spain suffered terribly during the 1940's. Prices spiraled, bread rationing continued until 1952, unemployment was high, and for five years from 1945 until 1950 the nation was plagued with drought. Drought in Spain means more than crop failure. It also means there is no electricity to provide power for the factories. Between 1945 and 1951 wages increased about 300 % while prices increased about 700 %. No wonder life looks grim on the stairway of *Historia*. Remembering the years of drought and the shortage of electricity, the man collecting for the light company and the complaints about the rising bill take on added meaning. And perhaps the presentation of blind students living comfortably in a modern school, enjoying life, thinking they are happy, developing their egoisms, contains a hidden irony.

Actually, the Spanish probably have the Korean War to thank for their increased prosperity. Although the United Nations returned to debate the status of Spain in 1949, and she began to receive some international recognition about then, world opinion still remained strongly anti-Spanish, not only because of her role in the Second World War, but because of her form of government. Harry Truman strongly denounced her as a dictatorship in June

of that year, and the United States turned down her requests
for financial assistance. In June of 1950 the Korean War
began. As fear of the communistic menace increased, public
opinion began to change. Franco reminded the world that
he had recognized the communistic threat back in the 30's,
and in November of that same year, five months after the
outbreak of hostilities, diplomatic relations were restored
with the United States. That same year the United Nations
lifted its diplomatic ban against Spain. After that it was
only a question of time until most other Western nations
recognized her government and diplomatic relations were
restored. Loans from the United States for agriculture
and other forms of foreign aid soon followed. But in
spite of this turn of events, Germany still remained the
favorite of the Franco government.

Foreign aid plus an end to the drought stimulated
industrial activity within Spain. Construction was started
on new hydroelectric plants. A cabinet shake-up in 1951
gave more importance to the monarchistic element within
the country and played down the power of the Falangists.
But life still remained extremely difficult for the average
Spaniard. Workers protested high living costs, inflation
continued, and housing lagged far behind the needs of the
nation.

We can see some of this reflected in *Tejedora* and
Señal. In *Tejedora* the country is devastated as the result
of Ulysses' absence in the war and the exploitation of the
country by the suitors residing in the palace under the guise
of diplomatic courtesy. The symbolic minded might say
Ulysses represents the exiled intellectual elements of
Spanish society, and the poaching suitors, the German and
later American forces which strongly influenced events

within the country. The status of the man on the street may be symbolized in Penélope, dreaming new dreams each day to rip them out each night, as life goes on, one day after another, with bread rationing, the palace becoming more run down all the time, and nobody apparently doing anything to improve the situation. Bread rationing actually continued in Spain until well into 1952.

The relationship between the social situation and *Señal* is once again ironic, as with *Ardiente*. Luis, the engineer, instead of working, relaxes at home in the country with his wife. The characters are so wrapped up in themselves they cannot work, and the nation continues far away in the remote distance, crippled by poverty, while the educated talents that could free it lie idle. Luis cannot exert himself to build the needed roads, apartment houses, and hydroelectric plants until he loses his wealth, until financial necessity forces him to work to contribute something to the well-being of his nation. Likewise the philosopher and the musician live apart from the suffering of the masses, part of the 17 % of the population receiving 2/3 of the national income. No wonder Buero instead of seeing tragedy in these lives sees only moral corruption. And when these conditions continue after he deplores them, one can understand why he says the direct social value of a play upon an individual is extremely limited.

I fail to see much direct influence of the political situation in the plays presented during 1953, *Casi un cuento de hadas* and *Madrugada,* but this lack may in itself be an indication of something. In 1952 the United States Sixth Fleet visited Spain for the first time since 1936, and instead of seeing German troops in the streets, the Spanish began to see Americans. Catholic religious leaders expressed concern over the dangers of Protestant proselytizing that could result from the influx of Americans. In 1953 Franco announced he would continue to serve as leader of the government as long as he lives, and in August of that year, a new Concordat between Spain and the Vatican was concluded. This Concordat provided that Catholicism would be taught in all the schools and that the Spanish government would participate in the naming of bishops. The economy began to improve, and Spain was admitted to UNESCO. *Casi un cuento de hadas* and *Madrugada* may express an optimism that things will be better, but more likely they represent a lack of freedom of expression which forces the author to turn to psychological themes.

In September, 1953, a defense pact was signed with the United States, and in 1954 the first contracts were let for construction of American air bases in Spain. The Spanish government itself considers 1953 a key year in its economic recovery, but in so doing fails to mention the effect the military pact with the United States had upon the economy. [5] According to these agreements the Americans were to use as much Spanish labor and materials as possible for the construction of the air bases in order to stimulate the economy. However, the Americans found Spain still in the horse and buggy days. Most Spaniards had never even seen modern construction tools, to say nothing about knowing how to use them. Complying with the terms of the agreement involved training Spanish workers and trying to get them to adapt to American

---

[5] See the official government commentary on this "año clave" in *España semanal,* 197 (July 18, 1966), p. 5.

working procedures. Construction of the bases was one
long frustration for both the Americans and the Spanish.
At times this resulted in a strong anti-American senti-
ment, but at the same time it opened new horizons in
Spanish thinking. Spanish workers began to demand more
in the way of material benefits.

In spite of this, during 1954 and 1955 life was still
difficult for the Spanish people. A severe power shortage
in 1954 forced industry to work at only 30 % of capacity.
The housing shortage continued acute, and Spain requested
more U.S. aid. About this time the anti-clerical feeling
within the country began to increase. In January, 1954,
the Catholic newspaper *Ecclesia,* the only paper in the
nation not under government control, complained that
the majority of workers were not practicing Catholics and
blamed Marxism and poverty. Since then if the anti-clerical
feeling has not become stronger, it has at least become
more open.

Hoy es fiesta shows this continued poverty, but this
time the author wonders if perhaps he should not have
more hope, and perhaps if his characters had dreamed
bigger dreams in the past, they could have accomplished
more. The play also reflects a growing indifference to
religious institutions as the characters look to the cards
for their future. Forgotten political prisoners are remembered through subtle references to Manola's husband, who
is in jail for unexplained reasons.

Las cartas boca abajo seems to resolve affirmatively
the doubt expressed in *Fiesta* as to whether the characters
could have done more to improve their situation as Buero
points out their moral corruption and shows how prejudices
and hatreds can be imagined and become fixed into behavior

patterns which an individual cannot escape. Hope here
lies in careful self-examination and continued striving for
moral improvement.

These years of economic improvement found a lessening
of police state terror and more public expression of interest
in the government by the citizens. In 1955 rumors circulated that Franco would have an operation. Juan Carlos
entered the Military Academy in Spain to complete his
education. With Juan Carlos' arrival in Spain the monarchistic elements within the country increased their activities.
During August of 1957 they began publication of *Realeza,*
a magazine dedicated to restoration of the monarchy. The
Law of Succession passed in 1947 states that Franco's
government shall be succeeded by a monarchy, the leader
of which must be male, over thirty years of age, and
Catholic. In 1933 Don Jaime had given up his claims
to the throne in favor of his brother Don Carlos, but in
1949 he renounced this renunciation. The question now
remained as to which one of the pretenders would be
favored. Since Juan Carlos was being educated in Spain,
many felt that he was being groomed for the job and
that it would go to either him or to his father. Various
communications between Franco and Don Juan added to
these speculations. Early in 1958 rumors circulated that
Franco was ailing and would soon go into exile.

The year 1957 also saw the nation undertake a fifteen
year program of expanded irrigation, electrification, for-
estation, colonization, etc. Unrest within the country was
high because of censorship, the rising cost of living, the low
level of Spanish gold dollar reserves, and many felt that
a behind the scenes battle was brewing between government
proponents of socialism and capitalism. Towards the end

of 1958 a financial scandal came to light which indicates the acute unrest within the country. More than 1,263 business men and politicans were discovered buying dollars on the black market and depositing them in Swiss banks. Since they were supporters of Franco, upon being discovered they were fined 25 % of the value and told they would receive a favorable rate of exchange for the rest. While all this was going on and many anti-Franco citizens were hoping for a change, the United States supported the foundering government with a seemingly endless stream of loans and foreign aid grants.

Buero's favorable portrayal of Carlos III in *Soñador* led the monarchistic elements within the country to believe he was supporting their cause. This was not the case. He wrote the play in defense of the enlightened policies of the 18th century, which Spanish authorities have not permitted to be fully investigated, along with the reign of Carlos III.

When Buero portrayed Felipe IV equally faithfully in *Las Meninas* as he really was, a despot, the monarchists felt he had turned against them. This difference in treatment can be explained by remembering that Buero seeks to express the truth. He questions and doubts everything, and sooner or later he is likely to show the other side of whatever argument is being presented. *Soñador* was written in a moment when hopes were high for a return of the king, and *Las Meninas* when Spanish intellectuals were trying very hard to obtain more freedom of expression.

The year 1958 also saw the beginning of a long period of strikes in Asturias. Labor unrest had been apparent for several years in the northern provinces, but now it reached such proportions that a new labor law outlining provisions for collective bargaining, the first in twenty-five years, was drafted. When Buero decided to write about the riots in *Soñador* he may have been thinking about labor's right to strike and to resist changes opposed upon them by an outside force. Valindin's confiscation of David's violin in *Concierto* also has something in common with the lockouts workers experienced from time to time during periods of labor unrest.

The twelve day strike in March of the Asturian coal miners started apparently because eight miners were laid off for lack of work. It grew in intensity until at one point 10,000 miners were involved. Two days before the strike ended the government suspended constitutional rights in all parts of Spain. Although the grievance appears chiefly economic, the police chose to attribute it to the communists. The communists seem to be the goat for just about everything in Spain. Nearly eighty persons were arrested in all, with some of them subjected to psychological and physical torture. Among those arrested one attempted suicide and two of them lost their minds. The economic situation worsened as the year progressed, with more arrests in Asturias. 1959 saw threats of a general strike.

During these years agitation for freedom of expression increased. Some Protestant churches were closed in 1958, and Protestant leaders tried to get them reopened. The Charter of the Franco government says that "no other external ceremonies or manifestations than those of the Catholic religion shall be permitted" and that "no one shall be molested for his religious beliefs or in the private practice of his worship." In actual practice, however, Protestants cannot hold government jobs, teach school, or be officers in the Armed Forces. Protestants are rarely

promoted in their work. Of the approximately 250 Protestant chapels in Spain at that time, only about 40 had
written authorization to hold services. The British government supported the Spanish Protestants in their attempts to obtain more freedom to worship. In contrast
with this tightening up of Protestant worship, Madrid's
Jewish Community in 1959 held Rosh Hashana services
in a regular synagogue for the first time since 1492.
About 150 attended.

In addition to this increased agitation for religious
freedom, Catholic groups began to speak out about other
aspects of civil liberties. *Ibérica* in 1959 reviewed the
various forms of government and ecclesiastical censorship.
Toward the end of the year a petition with 15,000 sig-
natures asking amnesty for political prisoners was presented
to the Spanish *Cortes*. In a pastoral letter dated January
15, 1960, twelve Archbishops appealed for greater social
justice in carrying out economic reforms and more just
distribution of goods to lessen social class distinctions.
When a riot occurred during Franco's visit to Barcelona
in the spring, 342 Basque priests in a letter to their bishops
denounced police brutality and violation of civil rights in
breaking up the demonstration and in making arrests.
The priests charged the government with arresting political
enemies without charges, holding them without trial,
torturing innocent citizens, and using a "superpropaganda"
machine to "deform" public opinion. Their protests were
quieted down, but two additional protests by lawyers
were made against police brutality in Catalonia. One was
by the Barcelona Bar Association, and the other by an
unnamed group. This marked the first protest in twenty-
one years by a professional group.

The end of the year saw more than 240 writers, scientists, and publishers writing the Minister of Education, Jesús Rubio, and the Minister of Information, Gabriel Arias Salgado, formally requesting a relaxation of press censorship and a clarification of the confusing restrictions on writers. International groups were also investigating the question of civil rights in Spain.

In considering this unrest and discontent expressed over the civil rights question, one should remember that civil rights as they are understood in the United States are almost incomprehensible to many Spaniards. By American standards, Spanish demands on the whole are extremely conservative, and the idea of society sacrificing itself for an individual completely escapes them. Even in Buero, one of the most progressive of Spanish thinkers, the individual always sacrifices himself for society, and not vice versa.

Nevertheless, we find the question of civil rights appearing in *Las Meninas* with a strong plea for freedom of expression. The effects of oppression are pointed out through the postrayal of the Negro slave and the hypocrisy of Velazquez' friends.

The year 1961 is more or less a year of continued unrest which sees the release of some political prisoners, continued interest in the treatment of political prisoners on the behalf of a group of international lawyers, a condemnation of Spanish censorship by British writers, a declaration supporting the Spanish working classes signed in Brussels by the International Confederation of Free Trade Unions and the International Confederation of Christian Trade Unions, a conference in Paris in the spring to see about obtaining amnesty for political prisoners, and increased opposition to Franco within the country by the Army. But that his power remained strong is evident by such acts as the passing of a law requiring all university officials to swear allegiance to the regime and the placing of 121 more books on the forbidden list.

This continued unrest with little to show for it in the way of actual material benefits finds Buero returning to the theme of blindness in *El concierto de San Ovidio*. The turbulent Spanish scene lies within the turbulent heart of David, who wants to love, work, and do all the things people living in a free society do, but unable to do them because of the oppression of a tyrant. In his blindness David sees no way to free himself.

In spite of this despair, Franco did yield somewhat to the unrest prevalent in the country, and the cabinet reshuffle on July 10, 1962, which left Manuel Fraga Iribarne as the new Minister of Information and Tourism led to a genuine censorship relaxation. This reshuffle apparently came in direct response to numerous clamors for social justice, agrarian reform, and European integration. July 13 the new minister, Manuel Fraga Iribarne, called a press conference to advise the public that Pope John XXIII's encyclical "Mater et Magistra" would be the future guide in social matters. This marked the first attempt by the Franco government to inform the public of government objectives. Iribarne immediately began to draft a new censorship law, the first since 1938, and marked relaxation of censorship has been noted since then. This more relaxed climate made possible the staging of both *El concierto de San Ovidio* (Nov. 16, 1962) and *Aventura en lo gris* (Oct. 1, 1963). *Concierto*, well received by both critics and the public, had a short run in a small,

not too well-known theater. *Aventura* was warmly received by the public on opening night but received un-
favorable reviews and lasted only a short time.

In the spring of 1962 the Asturian miners began a
series of strikes which extended throughout the summer.
Adequate press coverage of the strikes seemed to indicate
Iribarne's sincerity in relaxing censorship. There was no
violence and only ten people were arrested. Towards the
end of the summer it seemed the strike was wearing itself
out. These strikes had extended throughout Spain involving
some 170,000 workers from almost every industry.

Things remained more or less quiet until the following
summer of 1963 when new strikes broke out in Asturias.
This time the strikes continued into the fall when about
30 % of the mining force was out. Although the causes
are not clear, the chief points of contention seem to have
been dissatisfaction with government-run trade unions,
vested interests of government officials and agencies, dou-
ble-cross of an agreement reached in the spring, and en-
couragement by Catholic labor organizations. Remembering
the strikes of the previous year and fully aware of the
importance of coal in the national economy of a power
hungry nation, the government reacted to two petitions
signed by intellectuals, including Buero Vallejo, protesting
police atrocities in Asturias with derogatory publicity in
the press, radio, and television, threatening phone calls,
anonymous letters, and cancellation of contracts. One petition was sent before the presentation of *Aventura* and
the other afterwards. Although it cannot be proved, this
adverse publicity may have contributed to the limited success of the play and Buero's inability to stage his work
during succeeding theatrical seasons. But Buero is not

alone. Others, such as Sastre and Olmo, found it virtually impossible to present an original work during these first years of relaxed censorship. During the last half of 1966 the situation began to ease somewhat, but at the time of this writing, April, 1967, Buero's original writings still remain absent from the National theaters and television. [6]

---

[6] *El tragaluz* opened October 7, 1967, in the *Bellas Artes* theater, where it completed a very successful season. It was Buero's first original play to be presented since *Aventura* in 1963. *El sueño de la razón,* a very popular play based on the life of Goya, premiered in the Autumn of 1969.

TRAGIC TENDENCY

P R O B A B L Y there are almost as many definitions of tragedy as there are people who take the time to think about the subject. Buero himself has clearly stated his views on this from time to time, and in order to clarify his attitude, I will summarize what he wrote in an article published in 1958 in *El teatro: Enciclopedia del arte escénico* edited by Guillermo Díaz-Plaja.

Buero begins explaining his concept of tragedy by stating that about all tragedies down through the years have had in common is a certain emotion which could be defined in a thousand ways according to the example chosen. Then he continues to consider the functional effect of tragedy, catharsis, basing his discussion on Aristotle.

Tragic catharsis for him is the awakening of our strongest human impulses so they can be modified or pacified by means of projection to the dramatic work. Aristotle defined the emotions projected as terror and pity, and Buero interprets this to mean that after these emotions are projected, they become converted into "reflexive compassion before the evil of the world, and sacred terror."

As to the question of the type of spiritual elevation
catharsis can bring, he says:

Cathartic action can leave us passive or provoke within us the
imperative desire to work for the benefit of our fellow men
and against the sorrows or problems which the work presents.
But, however we respond, it elevates us. If it moves us to act,
it does so after raising us to a platform, ethical or philosophical, but consisting, and let us not forget it, not because of
explicit considerations or moralizations, although they may also
be in the work, but by the exemplary force of the plot and its
passions. Expressed in another way: by direct aesthetic impression and not argumentative, for aesthetic beauty is a supreme
discovery of man which by its mere presence can express all
while saying nothing.... In short, catharsis is the same as
interior improvement. [1]

-----

[1] P. 67. Bearing in mind that Greek scholars have no re-
liable text from which to translate the *Poetics* and that Buero
was working from a Spanish translation, it is interesting to compare his comments with these sections as translated by Benjamin
Jowett and Thomas Twining (New York: The Viking Press,
1957).

Tragedy, then, is an imitation of some action that is important,
entire, and of a proper magnitude, by language, embellished and
rendered pleasurable, but by different means in different parts
— in the way, not of narration, but of action — effecting through
pity and terror the correction and refinement of such passions.
(Chapter I, p. 230)

For the fable should be so constructed that, without the assistance of the sight, its incidents may excite horror and com-
miseration in those that hear them only... Since, therefore, it
is the business of the tragic poet to give that pleasure which
arises from pity and terror, through imitation, it is evident that
he ought to produce that effect by the circumstances of the
action itself. (Chapter XIII, p. 239)

Although the primary function of catharsis is the purification of emotions, this does not exclude the ethical. Tragedy tries to show that the catastrophies result from human errors with the final and greatest moral result an act of faith. It wants to lead the spectator to believe the catastrophe was justified and had a meaning although it may be impossible to conceive in any way what it might be. A play which leaves only a concern for social problems is not a tragedy.

Although the characters often suffer terrible misfortunes, tragedy is pessimistic only in the sense that it recognizes the darker aspects of the problems presented.

It represents in the field of art an heroic act by which man tries to understand suffering. It plants the possibility of overcoming it without submitting to the idea that suffering and the world from which it springs may be arbitrary facts. There is no pessimism more radical than that of accepting as fact the lack of meaning for the world, and there is no theatrical genre which seeks it more persistently—when it does not affirm it—than the tragic. . . . For tragedy invites us to that vital attitude that does not fear confronting the greatest horrors, and proposes to us that we acquire sufficient boldness to acquire a positive position from them. [2]

To illustrate and clarify the questions inherent in his comments, Buero discusses the works of Aeschylus, Sophocles, and Euripides. He explains how these authors begin and end their plays with an act of free will. The final act rectifies preceding errors and overcomes fate. As to the cause of the act of free will which brought about positive solutions at the end of the play, Buero says:

---

[2] P. 75.

The works cited clarify this. The protagonist knows or comes to learn through the fecund lesson of suffering the liberating force of reflection. By its exercise he comes to disbelieve the inexorability of fate and to depend upon his own rectifying capacity. This contemplation of fate with new eyes could also increase within him confidence in help from heaven. And in accordance with its own laws, heaven cannot remain permanently indifferent before an act of profound and living faith. [3]

That tragedy ends in faith explains why it cannot be pessimistic. Although an author may write a work which seemingly contains no faith, nevertheless it cannot be completely lacking, for if the author had absolutely no faith, he would not have had sufficient energy to have written the work.

Simply expressed, tragedy for Buero is an expression of "the faith that doubts." He clarifies this returning once again to Aeschylus, Sophocles, and Euripides. Aeschylus expresses profound faith; Sophocles, a firm believer also, places his faith more in man than in dogmas; and Euripides is what we would today call an agnostic. Tragedy moves between the points of these three men—the faith of Aeschylus, the doubt of Euripides, and the hope of Sophocles which links the two. All tragic conception exists within the triangle formed by faith, hope, and doubt. Pure faith and absolute negation do not exist. Doubt represents the vacilation between these two opposing poles.

Buero finishes his article saying:

And if men are not completely blind, they will continue taking valuable lessons from tragedy which will serve them to understand with good spirit and to affront with invincible valor the

---

[3] P. 73.

great truth from the mouth of Promethius which has been
handed down to us through the years: "Sorrow walks, always
wandering, and is felt at the turn of the feet of each one." [4]

Tragedy expresses the enigma of human existence—the
conflict between the ideology of predestination and free
will, between personal liberty and social necessity. It portrays the tension caused by these conflicts, ending in hope
or faith, whether at the social or transcendental level. But
without doubt there is no tragedy. And finally, Buero's
faith, as he himself has stated, is not faith in the religious,
theological sense, but rather a faith in the final resolution
of the conflicts.

Because the essence of life for Buero is tragic, he has
not limited himself to write tragedies which contain only
strong, forceful protagonists, or tragedies which follow any
preconceived idea of form or style. Tragic tension permeates his lighter social and experimental works as well
as those containing catastrophic events.

I like to think of tragedy in a slightly different manner than Buero. For me, tragedy represents the expression
of the myths which precede the formation of theological
or philosophical thought. Because these myths precede the
formation of thought, tragedy is abstract, indefinable, and
can be interpreted in a variety of ways. When a dramatic
work can be said to express a philosophical or theological
idea, it has moved from the field of tragedy to the field
of didactic literature. While Buero's work contains a very
strong moral tendency and at times clearly expresses the
ideas of the author, still no conclusive theological or

---

[4] P. 78.

philosophical thesis is contained. Because of this lack, his work for me is essentially tragic. It expresses the period of doubt and restlessness preceding the formation of conclusions, and as a result, must be approached subjectively as well as intellectually. It cannot be summarized or completely analyzed by any one person or in any one piece of writing.

THE TRANSCENDENTAL ASPECT

BUERO AND UNAMUNO

A L T H O U G H one can easily see in Buero's writing the influence of the two great 20th century Spanish philosophers, José Ortega y Gasset and Miguel de Unamuno, the influence of Unamuno seems to be the stronger in spite of the fact that Buero avoids Unamuno's passionate outbursts and expresses himself through a literary style which more nearly resembles the cold, calculating logic of Ortega.

The aspect most Unamunesco is the numerous paradoxes. Like Unamuno, Buero strives to make his readers think, to create questions within their minds, to leave them feeling a little less self-satisfied, and to stimulate them to ponder the deepest transcendental questions of all time. Unamuno pointed out the impossibility of being a Christian, and Buero does somewhat the same, but in a different way. So while it is in the approach to an understanding of Christianity that one finds the greatest similarities between the two, it is also here where one finds the greatest differences.

Whether Unamuno was a Christian or not, nobody really knows. Because of the paradoxes within his work, one can prove almost anything. I myself feel he was a man of tremendous faith who, because of his great intellect, could see more than the usual number of facets to the numerous questions he considered. The paradoxes and apparent conflict which appear within his work spring not so much from a lack of faith, although undoubtedly like all humans he suffered moments of despair and doubt, as from the firm conviction that faith begins with doubt. He dedicated himself to creating these doubts, believing they would eventually evolve into faith.

Unlike Unamuno, Buero expresses doubts which at the present time have not crystallized into faith in the religious sense, but rather remain in the form of a hope within the author's mind. He intellectually explores his problems hoping to find a black and white answer, knowing full well that the answers to transcendental questions exceed man's reasoning powers. He represents intellectual activity during a period of spiritual vacuum when traditional myths no longer suffice and man looks for up-to-date theological or philosophical thought. By the very nature of their numerous contradictions and at times lack of explicitness, Buero's writings express the vital, living myths of our time. Unamuno recognized the need for re-evaluation of Christian thought. Buero explores the different possibilities for supplying that need.

Another important difference between Unamuno and Buero lies in the relationship of the individual to society. Unamuno found it impossible to be a Christian principally because of the way in which society interpreted Christianity. An overwhelming sense of guilt provides Buero's

greatest stumbling block. In one the obstacle lies outside
the individual; in the other, within.

POETRY AND MYTH

In spite of Buero's strong intellectual approach, his
writings contain much of the poetic and mythic. Not only
words, but also lights and music help create the aesthetic
impression—to show the passage of the day, the coming
out of the stars, the beauty of the ethereal. And as mentioned in the commentary on *Señal*, Buero himself has
stated that through the use of music in *Señal, Concierto,*
and *Tejedora,* he has tried to indicate his recognition of
the limitations of the word. When Buero does not resort
to the poetic and the aesthetic to express the inexpressable,
he falls back on doubts, intellectual conflicts, which at
times the critics call "confusion."

The public has not always responded too well to these
efforts to enter the world of the poetic. Whether such
commercial failures represent true failures or whether they
represent works too advanced for the audience which
viewed them is debatable.

In *Ardiente,* his first work, this attempt to penetrate
the mythic expresses itself in a lack of logic. To say one
should reject a comfortable, well-organized modern school
which attempts to teach blind children to lead constructive
lives is pure nonsense, unless one forgets logic and enters
the mythic world which excludes human reason. Here the
results of the author's efforts were successful.

They were not so successful, however, in terms of
audience reaction in *Casi un cuento de hadas* where Buero

tried to unveil the truths inherent within a fairy tale for children. He forgot one very important factor—children have an intuition which adults do not possess, and as a result their stories possess truths which remain forever incomprehensible to adult minds. One of the world's greatest mysteries is that an adult can hide all his tensions and worries from adult companions, but an infant child, perhaps still a babe in arms, can sense this inner conflict. As a child matures and becomes a rational individual, his egoism develops and he loses this sensibility; the world of childhood recedes from that of adulthood. Converting the truths of a children's story into sophisticated adult entertainment presents a playwright with one of his greatest challenges.

Another questionable success was *Irene, o el tesoro,* the story of frustrated motherhood. Here Buero turned again to the poetic, to elves and colored lights. This world of fantasy fused with his cold logic provides a strange contrast with the logic a little heavy perhaps for the fragility of the poetry.

In *Aventura,* a play not too well received by the public but in my opinion definitely one of the best, he resorts even more to the poetic. One can analyze the play logically and try to figure out what he is talking about, but to do so frequently leads to a blind alley as far as rational thought is concerned, and diminishes the aesthetic impression. The play is much more appealing if interpreted as a modern, poetic interpretation of Calderon's "life is a dream" theme. Rational twentieth century audiences are not used to viewing poetic expressions of this type, and only time can judge their true merits.

INTELLECTUAL CONCEPTS

Leaving to one side the poetic aspect of his work, let us now consider Buero's intellectual conception of the transcendental, beginning with man and the universe.

Considering first the "life is a dream" theme, we find this appearing again and again throughout his work. What are the limits of human reality and dreams? His plays are full of references to the living dead. In *Tejedora* Ulysses kills Anfino, but Anfino lives as a positive influence while Ulysses is spiritually dead. Penélope says that in order to find peace one needs the universal word of love which one finds in death. In a dramatic scene in *Soñador* Esquilache tells Ensenada he is lost because he has not lived for anything outside himself for years. In *Aventura* to learn to dream would be to learn to live. When Pilar dies in *Fiesta,* she says it is like a great joy enveloping her. Reality, for her husband, seems like a dream. Death as portrayed on the stage by Buero is not a terrible end, but rather a beautiful beginning, a resolution of existing conflicts and doubts.

At the same time Buero does not conceive eternity in traditional Catholic terms. He himself, although reared a Catholic, has left the Church. This does not mean he has rejected the Christian faith, for, as he says, too many people have unsuccessfully tried through the years to destroy it. He is careful to add that he views the eternal not in traditional theological terms, but rather as a resolution of conflicting forces.

Buero envisions human events not as the direct result of cause and effect but rather of a complex series of relationships. *Señal* most clearly expresses this idea. Failing to understand the author's viewpoint, critics have complained that he leads up to the point of presenting a "miracle" and then backs away to conclude it was merely a series of coincidences. To those accustomed to thinking along traditional dogmatic lines, this may seem somewhat of a letdown. In one sense it is, but at the same time it indicates a more progressive viewpoint. Buero, rather than denying the "miracle," points out that it actually exists, something many contemporary and even Christian thinkers might deny, and then continues to conclude that modern man, like those of the past, can not explain its occurrence. Miraculous incidences are just as miraculous as they ever were, but the author refuses to define them in theological or philosophical terms. This refusal to accept traditional theology in no way expresses a lack of faith, as the characterization makes quite clear. Enrique, the husband, possesses a personality which must express hope through doubts. His more passive wife, less intellectually inclined, can express her hopes through a more traditional manner of faith. But they are still only two ways of expressing the same thing.

In trying to discover a new, truer interpretation or understanding of those traditional values which have survived the ages, Buero looks to man himself, to his biology, and to his subconscious. The maternal and paternal instinct is found in each play, frequently explored within the family situation. Paradoxically, the instinct is often destroyed within the family situation only to appear between strangers, as between Ana, Silverio, and the baby in *Aventura*, and between David and Donato in *Concierto*. At times it appears between an individual and his work, as in the characterization of the musician Luis in *Señal*. This latter presentation is reminiscent of Unamuno, who talked of his literary creations as living entities and offspring.

Another aspect of Buero's exploration of the role of biology in human reality lies in the frequent inclusion of physical and psychic defects, including the famous theme of blindness. Man cannot always remove these defects, but as Buero states on his recording "Me llamo Antonio Buero Vallejo," through their acceptance man may develop the hope necessary to overcome them. And as I point out later in the remarks on *Cartas*, often man creates a defect where none exists.

The theme of blindness also indicates man's inability to understand and therefore his inability to correct his situation, a further exploration of the role of biology, or predestination, in human affairs. Additional comments about the theme of blindness are found in the sections on tragedy and in the discussions of his two great tragedies, *Ardiente* and *Concierto*. For Buero the heart of his work lies here.

In addition to considering the role of biology, Buero also probes human emotions to show the loves, hates, petty jealousies, greed, and personal ambitions of his characters. Some of his characters are genuinely good, as Irene; many are rebels, like Ignacio and David; and many others are petty and miserly, like Mauro. As a rule he develops his characters in depth in order to show the different facets of their emotional make-up and how these influence their behavior. In developing their psychologies he avoids the light treatment of immorality and the idealized, sticky sweet treatment of virtue and love so common in contemporary theater. The bad examples in his plays serve to help his spectators and readers understand and have compassion for their fellow man.

In consistently maintaining a high moral tone, Buero flees from conventional platitudes. Virtue may triumph, but it does so frequently culminating in death. Sacrifice dogs the heels of compassion. Joy lives with sorrow. Buero strives to inspire through his plays his viewer's spiritual improvement, but he possesses no illusions about man's virtue or its improvement by increased material benefits. As he indicates in *Ardiente,* humans do not love. They feel only egoism, a desire for flattery. If humans could love, he envisions this love as existing on an elevated plane detached from life's daily trivialities. This perfect or almost perfect individual capable of true love could accept whatever sorrow came his way for his spirit would be above misfortune. Its highest point would fuse with universal powers while its lowest would concern itself with daily chores.

I asked Buero how one could arrive at this almost perfect state, and he replied there are three ways: by works, by suffering, or by reflection. But regardless of the means, one must possess a feeling of guilt in order to pass through the "dark night" to find to "living flame of love." [1] He himself has not had that experience. During the experience of this "dark night" the individual would become aware of his guilt, or his sins.

For me this is the essence of Buero's work. Not in the theme of blindness as he maintains, but in the strong sense of guilt and the search for the "dark night." Ignoring the aspect of dramatic technique, the evolution of Buero's

---

[1] The reference here, of course, is to San Juan de la Cruz.

work seems greatest in his treatment of guilt whereas the other attitudes remain more or less stable.

Another question I put to Buero had to do with pure catastrophe. Does it exist? Buero said no. Everything can be explained by relationships of some sort, although man may not have any idea what that relationship might be. If it were possible to arrive at a point where the catastrophe could not be explained by relationships, it could be explained as punishment for sin. For Buero even a newborn baby is guilty. The guilt lies in those factors inherent within his nature which will cause him to commit immoral acts as he matures.

Buero states this idea perhaps most clearly in *Fiesta* when Silverio talks about the beast each one carries within himself, the beast which might spring to the fore at any unguarded moment and cause an individual to commit acts of unbelievable inhumanity. Silverio accepts the death of his wife as punishment for his own bestial acts in the past.

The ideas just expressed are difficult to reconcile with a faith that does not exist in a theological or religious sense, but rather as a final reconciliation of conflicting forces. A reconciliation of conflicting forces implies no moral connotations as traditionally conceived, and if there is one thing Buero's theater has above all else, it is a plea for morality.

Buero's indirect references to war, as in *Tejedora*, Ignacio's statement that he is going to bring the students war and not peace, the plot of *Aventura*, the riot in *Soñador*, and Silverio's jealousy in *Fiesta* because of the attack upon his wife by an enemy soldier seem to suggest that the inhumanities committed by civilized man between the years of 1936 and 1945 may stimulate this strong sense of guilt. In the last scene of *Cartas* Adela kneels before Anita and asks her forgiveness, confessing her guilt. Anita turns and walks away as the shrieks of the birds invade the room. This magnificent scene shows the strength of this sense of guilt. Whether Buero himself feels guilty or whether this characteristic of his writing indicates only a critical attitude is another question. Probably it does both of these things.

At times Buero's players express repentance by sacrificing themselves, as in *Soñador* and in *Aventura,* or by admitting that their misfortunes have resulted from their own misdeeds as a form of punishment, as in the aforementioned example of *Fiesta.* However, I feel these resolutions represent an intellectual attempt to portray the "noche oscura," and as yet Buero has not resolved this problem of guilt within his theater.

Sophocles had much the same problem, and he wrote three plays at three different times of his life to wrestle with it. The first one, the *Antigone,* like the first of Buero's great tragedies of the blind, *Ardiente,* is a search for values, a presentation of the conflict between idealism and practicality.

The second, *Oedipus the King,* shows an intelligent man who wants to do what is right, can not do so, and blinds himself as punishment. In Buero's second tragedy of the blind, *Concierto,* David tries to do what is right, can not, and is hung as punishment for his crime. This second great tragedy by Buero reflects a greater spirit of resignation than *Ardiente,* and the forces of the universe in contrast with the efficacy of human endeavors seem more powerful. This same shift in relative power occurs in Sophocles.

In Sophocles third treatment of the Oedipus myth, *Oedipus at Colonus*, he finds the burden of guilt too great. The Gods whisk Oedipus away after he shouts his innocence. Life for Oedipus had been some sort of a "catharsis" with the reason for it all unknown. Or in other words, it had been one long "dark night." Only time will tell us how Buero's third great tragedy will end.

ANALYSES OF PLAYS

HISTORIA DE UNA ESCALERA

Historia de una escalera, the great success which insured
Buero a permanent place in the history of Spanish literature, portrays not only the modern theme of man caught
in time unable to free himself, but also shows a culture
trying to rebuild itself. Buero takes his characters from
the humbler walks of life—extremely poor people with
almost no resources for improving their lot other than
their hopes. When the work was written, Spain also had
almost no resources, only hope.

The plot is very simple. Two generations meet each
other on the stairway of a Madrid tenement on three different days during their lifetime. Ten years pass between
the first and second act, and twenty years between the
second and third. The third act finds the younger generation on the stairway expressing the same hopes and
dreams of the future expressed in the first act by their
parents.

Although nothing really happens in the play, it is a
masterpiece of careful dramatic construction. The three
acts parallel each other to a certain extent in dramatic
form but without becoming tedious. Buero resembles

Benavente in this technical aspect, although their dramatic attitudes are completely different. Each character is carefully and individually portrayed. Buero has said that he knows these kinds of people, and their lifelike descriptions seem to confirm he does.

Because of the poltical scene at the time and Buero's own background, some critics have tended to overemphasize the political symbolism that the work may contain and neglect the more universal and human qualities. Of course they are correct in considering the political relevance, for a work of art always expresses a conflict between the artist and his environment. And has been already pointed out, Buero is extremely conscious of the political situation within the country.

William L. Shelnutt in his article "Symbolism in Buero's *Historia de una escalera*" published in *Hispania* in March, 1959, develops a very interesting interpretation, although exaggerated, of the political symbolism inherent in the play. He claims Buero is restating the conflicts of the Generation of '98, namely, where to, Spain, and by what means. The old tumble-down house represents Spain, and man in the play represents the soul or spirit of Spain. The family relationships of son, father, daughter, etc. represent the selfish interests which keep Spain from being a great nation. The two young men, Fernando and Urbano, represent the Spanish intellectuals who lead the country, talk big, and do nothing. Elvira, whom Fernando marries because of her money, represents extreme individuality and selfishness. Carmina, who loves Fernando and marries Urbano, represents love of her fellow man and the ability to work for the common good. Doña Asunción is the poor nobility and Don Manuel the common man who through work has made something of himself. Shelnutt continues like this to designate an aspect of Spanish life for each character.

In the sense that Spain is a composite of the people and the people contain all these characteristics, he is justified in his interpretation. He overlooks, however, that Buero's characters are first of all people with all the complexities of human personality, and secondly symbols. Buero writes a "personal" theater before he writes a "political" one. His characters live in a political or social situation which influences and limits their activities, as Buero lives in a political situation which limits his activities and causes him to write in this manner. Expressed in a different way, the human elements transcend the political.

Jean Paul Borel gives a different interpretation of the political aspect. [1] For him *Historia* presents the tensions created in a society which imposes conformity upon its members. As the characters were chained to the stairway and could not determine their destiny, so the political situation in Spain limited the freedom of its citizens. With this interpretation the characters remain complex human individuals instead of abstract symbols.

Unless the symbolism is obvious, I prefer to think of the tensions, conflicts, and different aspects of the problems presented rather than say that this or that represents some certain thing. This allows a more open interpretation, and each reading of the play offers new meanings. The stairway in *Historia*, for example, can symbolize the government, poverty, human personality, fate, society, or all of these things.

---

[1] "Buero Vallejo: Teatro y Política," 226-234.

The main theme of the play, rather than political, seems to be that of man caught in time unable to escape. At the beginning of the play Fernando, one of the young men, says:

It isn't that, Urbano. It's that I'm afraid of time! That's mostly what makes me suffer. To see how the days pass, and the years... without anything changing. Only yesterday you and I were two youngsters who came up here to hide and smoke our first cigarettes... That was ten years ago! We've grown up without realizing it, going up and down the stairs, always surrounded by our parents who don't understand us, by neighbors who talk about us, and then we talk about them... Looking for a thousand ways out and humiliating ourselves in order to pay the rent, the light... and the potatoes. And tomorrow, or within ten years that can pass like a day, as these last ten have passed... It would be terrible to continue this way! Going up and down the stairway, a stairway that doesn't lead anywhere, tampering with the light meter, hating work, losing day after day. (p. 19)

Thirty years later at the end of the third act Urbano says much the same thing.

And what have your big plans about your work come to? You haven't known how to do anything more than look down your nose at others. But you haven't emancipated yourself; you haven't freed yourself! You're still chained to this stairway like me, like everybody. (p. 64)

The relationship between the first and second acts offers another example. In the first act Fernando challenges Urbano to see who can go the furthest in life during the next ten years. The second act occurs after the ten years have lapsed. Fernando and Urbano are older, family situations have been modified by births and deaths, but the stairway looks exactly the same as it did ten years previously, with Fernando and Urbano still going up and down.

A final parallel exists in two speeches by Fernando, Senior and Fernando, Junior. At the end of the first act Fernando, Senior tells Carmina, the girl he loves, that he will work, become an expert draftsman, and eventually an engineer. At the end of the third act his son tells Carmina's daughter almost exactly the same thing. Time has trapped the residents of the tenement with each new generation repeating the same old dreams.

Although this use of time may seem pessimistic, it is by no means the whole story. The first and second acts show the happiness and saddness of life. The first act is the happy act. Elvira's father graciously pays the light bill for Fernando's mother. The neighbors gossip, and the young people are in love. A good-natured rivalry exists between Fernando and Urbano, and the act ends as Fernando and Carmina dream of the future. The second act is a sad act. It begins with Carmina and her mother weeping because of the death of her father. The act reveals that Fernando married Elvira for her money and both have been extremely unhappy. Rosita, another unfortunate young woman, married a drunken woman-chaser and her father will have nothing to do with her. As life destroyed in Fernando and Urbano the illusions of their youth, they became exceedingly jealous of each other. Urbano tries to cheer Carmina after the death of her father, but Elvira and Fernando express their condolences accompanied by cutting insinuations about Fernando's marriage to Elvira instead of Carmina.

The third act is a mixture of joy and sadness. The old tenants who have not died are still there, but new owners have taken over the building. When the old tenants are gone, they intend to renovate it. The characters remaining from the first act are bitter and lonesome, but their offspring are lively and hopeful. Hope accompanies youth, in spite of the stairway.

The idea just expressed could be expressed another way. The first act can be considered the act of faith, and the second, the act of doubt. The final act, which combines the spirit of the two previous, is the act of hope.

In addition, life on the stairway is a mixture of good and bad, but basically they are the same thing. Rosita, the unfortunate who married the drunkard, became reconciled with her family through the years. Her virtuous sister Trini, who had stayed at home and cared for the others, tells her:

TRINI: How equal you and I are at the bottom!
ROSA: At the bottom all we women are alike.
TRINI: Yes... You've been the scandal of the family, and I the victim. You wanted to live your life and I dedicated myself to the lives of others. You joined yourself with a man and I only know the smell of those at home. Now you see: at the end we've come to be equal failures. (p. 61)

Life on the stairway is the same for all, a mixture of laughter and tears, ambitions and disappointments, selfishness and sacrifice, good and bad.

But the question of escape from the stairway remains. Fernando in his youth had a theory: he would study and become a great success, all by himself. Urbano told him he could not do it. He needed the help of those around him. He, Urbano, would become a success by working with others through the union, and collectively they would make the world better for everybody. The end of the play finds Fernando an embittered white collar worker, and Urbano a resentful tradesman. Neither had found an escape from the stairway.

Perhaps no escape exists. Or perhaps these people are looking for the wrong thing. They seek material escape —enough money to pay the light bill and buy the potatoes. Perhaps the poor by themselves cannot escape from this stairway, from the oppression of poverty.

But there may be another escape. At the end of the play as the Fernando and Carmina of the new generation repeat the words their parents repeated thirty years previously, the Fernando and Carmina of the first act exchange glances. Both had married hoping to find financial security. In trying to free themselves from the chains of poverty, they found no escape and even less happiness. What would have happened if they had reconciled themselves to their humble existence and remained loyal to their love? Would that love have been strong enough to overcome poverty? If so, perhaps love may be the catalyst necessary to enable the younger generation to escape and make for themselves a new and better life.

So here, in perhaps the most pessimistic of Buero's plays, one finds the characters fighting against time, being crushed and embittered by the years. But in spite of everything, hope springs anew with each generation, a hope suggesting that man can overcome poverty, and that perhaps somewhere there in his dreams he may find happiness.

LAS PALABRAS EN LA ARENA

Las palabras en la arena, a short one-act play, dramatizes the story of Christ and the adultress. It was written for a competition among friends, a private tertulia, and later submitted in the competition for the award of the *Asociación de Amigos de los Quintero* in 1949. It won the award and was presented by the class of Declamation of the Conservatory in the Teatro Español.

Although the play is short, it possesses the same quality construction which characterizes Buero's other works, and like the others, portrays a morally corrupt hypocritical society. Noemi, the supposedly loyal wife, arranges a rendezvous with her lover during her husband's forthcoming absence. While she is doing this, her husband and his Jewish friends, a Pharisee, a Sadducee, and a scribe, witness Jesus' forgiveness of the adultress. In forgiving her, Jesus had written in the sand the cardinal sin of each one of the spectators. All deny their sin and laugh at the "Rabbi." For Noemi's husband Jesus had written "assassin," and he too laughs. A few minutes later, however, in a fit of passion when he learns of his wife's infidelity, he kills her. Each one of the characters in the play pretend to be something they are not, but Buero through his skill-ful manipulation of the plot not only reveals their true selves, but also their awareness of their hypocrisy.

Consideration of this play in conjunction with Buero's other work suggests several things about the author. First, it seems unlikely that the theme would have attracted him if he were as cool to the Christian faith as he would like people to believe. Also, it suggests that he cannot conceive Christianity as existing independently of moral values. And since this was one of his first plays and he never again returned to write about Christianity directly as such, it leads one to wonder if perhaps the reception he received when he returned to public life may not have done more to influence his religious and philosophical attitudes than the years in prison.

Technically speaking the play is excellent. Buero sketches his characters carefully and builds up the dra-matic tension until it climaxes at the very end of the play. It is indeed a graphic representation of one episode in the Christian tradition.

F O R Valbuena Prat this play expresses the confused frustrations of a "resentido," the frustrations of a person mad at the world who wants to make everybody else suffer because he is unhappy. In the sense that it is the outcry of an angry young man and at times may appear confused and obscure, I agree with him completely, but at the same time one should remember that this confusion, obscurity, and even anger, comprise the essence of the play. Our angry young man wants to know what life is all about.

Before trying to understand what Buero is saying in *Ardiente,* let us review for a moment the relationship that exists between doubt and faith. Ortega y Gasset has written that man exists within the relationship between himself and his environment. They are interdependent. Beliefs constitute the basis of this relationship, most of which man inherits, and all of which are given to him. He believes the sun will rise each morning, the ground will remain beneath his feet when he walks, and that when he lays something on the table, it will stay there instead of flying through the air. These beliefs are part of him; he cannot explain them, and by his will he cannot create them or take them away. For Ortega, they are the true or absolute reality.

When these beliefs come in contact with the environment, they may become doubts. In order to quiet these doubts, man thinks and creates ideas. He can do nothing else. These ideas are created in the imagination, and as a result, all ideas, poetic as well as scientific, are imaginative or fantastic. Man realizes this and he accepts them with varying degrees of faith. All faith is based upon doubt. Without doubt man would never be aware of his faith. [1] Buero in this play is fully conscious of the doubts presented and they torment him unmercifully to become the central theme of the work.

Buero's most tragic character, the one with the greatest doubts, is blind Ignacio of *Ardiente*. Ignacio knows there is a light and he cannot rest until he finds it. He wants to see the stars, and he knows that if he could see the stars, he would want to reach them. A rebel, he cannot content himself with the worlds created by men but must look forward into the universe. Doubt causes his discontentment. If he were not tormented by doubts, he could accept the rationalizations of his companions or create some equally satisfying of his own. Instead, his doubts lead him to destroy everything created by man and seek a greater truth.

Buero told me that when he named Ignacio he was thinking of Ignacio de Loyola, founder of the Society of Jesus during the Counter Reformation. This order was expelled from Spain during the 18th century and again

---

[1] *Ideas y creencias* (Madrid: Espasa-Calpe, S. A., 1964).

just prior to the Civil War. Ignacio resembles Loyola
during the early years of his search to know God, years
which found him crippled from the war, abandoning the
wealth and comfort of his home and wandering around
southern Europe for some ten years, ragged, living off
the charity of others, always seeking something more. After
founding the Society of Jesus Loyola changed. He became
obsessed with the importance of organization, respectability,
and healthful living. Buero's Ignacio changes also when he
falls in love, but he is killed before his searching can be
converted into material benefits.

Doubt exists not only in the character Ignacio but
throughout the entire play. The book begins with these
quotations:

> Y la luz en las tinieblas resplandece;
> mas las tinieblas no la comprendieron.
>
>   (Juan, 1-5)

> La sombra es el nidal íntimo, incandescente,
> la visible ceguera puesta sobre quien ama.
> Provoca los abrazos íntima, ciegamente,
> y recoge en sus cuevas cuanto la luz derrama.
>   (Miguel Hernández: *Hijo de la sombra*.)

The choice of words to differentiate the blind from the
seeing also indicates doubt. *Videntes* are those with sight.
The play defines this word to mean those with double
vision, or simply those who can see. The dictionary of
the Royal Academy defines it similarly and adds the
additional meaning of prophet.

Through the different characters Buero presents three
different attitudes towards man's ignorance of the mysteries

of the universe. First, Ignacio's, full of doubts and seeking a truth he knows in his heart he will find only in death. Another, that of Carlos, the practical man. He sees no need to worry about things one can do nothing about, because that only makes people restless and unhappy. Besides, everyone has his problems. Some are blind; others have bad hearts; or they get killed in the war. No-one should think his troubles are greater than anyone else's, but rather forget them. Miguel has a third attitude. For him everything is a joke. The world consists of his own personal experiences, and he refuses to admit anything else exists. Since he has never experienced sight, he concludes that those who think they see suffer a collective hallucination. He and those like him are the normal ones.

Ignacio replies to the arguments of Miguel and Carlos by telling them they have no right to live, because they will not accept life as it is, a mystery, and the suffering it brings, and try to probe its depths.

The conflict between Ignacio and the psychology of the school further accentuates these different approaches to life. Ignacio's inquiring mind compels him to seek the source of everything. He cannot accept something as truth merely because some teacher or adult tells him it is, or because it makes society's affairs more orderly. He wonders about his blindness, and in the following passage expresses the fundamental question found in Buero's dramatic work:

Then I sat down on a step and began to think. For the first time I tried to understand why I was blind and why there had to be blind people. It is abominable that the majority of people, without being any better than us, or doing anything to deserve it, should enjoy a mysterious power that emanates from their eyes and with which they can embrace us and stare at us without our being able to avoid it. We've been denied that power of apprehending things at a distance, and we're underdogs, for no reason at all, to those who live there on the outside. Maybe that old chant the blind used to say sitting on the street corners in our father's day asking alms: "There's no wealth like sight, dear brothers," doesn't fit in well with our tranquil student life, but I think it's more sincere and worthwhile. Because they didn't act like us; they didn't believe foolishly that they were normal. (p. 38)

If one had to select only one paragraph out of all Buero's writing to illustrate the essence of his work, this paragraph could probably do it best. Like Ignacio, Buero wonders why some people are more fortunate than others, to what extent man must accept his fate, and what he can do to control his destiny. He wonders about the suffering of the innocent, why there are social classes, and what in the universe transcends the understanding of mortal man. From these elementary questions evolve the theme of democracy, his attitude towards personal responsibility, his characterization, and so forth.

The philosophy of the school and its famous "morale of steel" represents the other side of this attitude. The students are brainwashed into thinking they are happy, and when unhappy Ignacio arrives, they try to brainwash him, too. Ignacio sees no reason to accept this "morale of steel" as true just because it sounds pleasant. Protesting the hypocrisy of the society in which he finds himself, he tells Carlos, "This Center is founded upon a lie.... The lie that we are normal beings." (p. 49) He sees the fear in the lives of the others which leads them to live a lie, and they see in him a malcontent, a bitter coward, refusing to abandon his cane. The question is, can man find comfort for his suffering in a truth he can never know, or must he depend upon a lie? I asked Buero this question, and he told me that if he had to choose, he would choose the truth, regardless of how painful it might be.

Paradoxically, Ignacio refuses to put his cane aside because he recognizes his weakness. The cane, he says, keeps him from stumbling. Actually he can walk as well without it as the others, but it represents his way of living with his doubts and fears. Refusing to rely exclusively upon his own resources, he insists upon outside help. And so very subtly the author raises the question of how much man can do relying exclusively on his own efforts.

In his search for truth and light, Ignacio comes to believe they exist. When he offers this faith to the others, they reject it. Their egoism worries him, and he would like to see the students find something of value outside themselves. A useful life to him means more than an orderly house and neat clothing. Slovenly dress accentuates his rebellion.

While Ignacio's attitude infects the others, at the same time they begin to influence him. When his doubts were greatest, he thought of suicide. Interest in and concern for the others lead him to abandon this idea. Falling in love with Juana supplies a reason to continue living.

But even love in this play is full of doubts. While love gives Ignacio's life purpose, the love between Carlos and Juana and Miguelín and Elisa seems to be no more than egoism. Ignacio suggests the blind Don Pablo married the sighted Doña Pepita because he needed someone to care for him, and she married him because she was too ugly to find anyone else.

Love is something marvelous. Carlos' and Juana's love, for example. But that marvel is no more than a sad parody of love

among the seeing! Because they possess the loved one completely. They can engulf him with a glance. We possess by pieces.
A caress, the momentary murmur of the voice... In reality we
don't love each other. We feel sorry for ourselves and try to
disguise that sad pity with happy nonsense calling it love. I think
it would be better if we wouldn't disguise it. (p. 45)

True love between blind humans does not exist — only
egoism. Buero believes this, and while not expressed as
implicitly as here, the attitude reappears again and again
in other works.

At the end of the play Carlos, consumed by jealousy,
kills Ignacio. Doña Pepita sees him move the body after
the murder. In telling Carlos she knows of his act she
agrees that the good of the school must be the first consideration of all. She does not punish him or betray his
crime to the others. Although she wants his confidence
and cannot obtain it, she does not interfere in the activities
of the blind boy. As Buero says, she sees but does nothing.

The weakness of the play as I see it lies in the
portrayal and lack of definition in Doña Pepita. Buero
has said she represents sterile prudence — the one who
can see but does not want to see, and because she does
not want to see, she can prevent nothing. She is all of
this, of course, but what if she had been different? On
the positive side, she tried to remove the suffering of the
blind and elevate their spirits. There is nothing wrong
with that. And if she had betrayed the crime, what would
she have accomplished? Her attraction to Carlos suggests she saw in him the son she never had and thought as
a mother, with her heart instead of her head. Probably the
most sublime of human loves is mother love, and Buero
may have been intending to show that even this is no

more than egoism, although for me that is not completely clear.

After Carlos kills Ignacio, Ignacio's friends abandon him and the school seems ready to return to the peaceful routine it knew before his coming. But as his love for the students had changed Ignacio, so does an unknown love found in death change Carlos. Practical Carlos, consumed by jealousy to the point of committing murder, becomes the dreamer, thinking of the stars and wanting to see them.

And now the stars are shining in all their splendor, and those who can see are enjoying their marvelous presence. Those far away worlds are there behind the window panes... Within reach of our sight...! if we had it... (p. 79)

LA TEJEDORA DE SUEÑOS

GREEK myths held a fascination for Buero from the time of his youth, and as early as 1949 he felt the urge to try his hand at adapting Homer's story of Ulysses and Penélope. Three years later he realized this desire. Valbuena Prat has described this play as "perhaps one of the best demonstrations of the renovation of a mythic theme of our time." [1]

In the myth as related in the *Odyssey*, Ulysses accompanies Agamemnon and Menelaus in their journey to capture Troy and recover Menelaus' wife, Helen, whom Paris had stolen from him. Ulysses returns nineteen years later after experiencing numerous hardships. During this time his wife, Penélope, remains faithful, mourning his absence, and more or less defenseless against the greed of those about her. Ulysses returns in disguise to find the palace full of drunken suitors trying to press Penélope into choosing a husband. After assuring himself of her fidelity, he reveals his identity and kills the suitors. Penélope greets him with open arms.

------

[1] *Historia del teatro español* (Barcelona: Editorial Noguer, S. A., 1956), p. 662.

Buero's play follows much the same general outline with a great many dramatic liberties. The greatest difference between the two works lies in Penélope's reception of Ulysses. During his absence Buero's Penélope has time to reflect about the justice of men leaving their homes and families to spend twenty years fighting for another man's wife, and concludes she hates all Ulysses and his absence stand for. Instead of eulogizing fidelity, Buero portrays the moral decay which occurs when an individual follows the path of least resistance and allows himself to be swept along by events.

La tejedora reflects serious study of classical literature on the part of the author. The first act reads like a 20th century version of the first part of Aeschylus' *Agamemnon*. Instead of having the watchman on the roof to set the tone of the play and explain what has been going on for the past twenty years, the play begins with a chorus of slaves reciting a chant extolling Penélope's virtue. Then, because 20th century appetites tend more towards dialogue than towards recitatives, the chorus breaks up into individual members who continue to explain the misfortunes which have befallen the palace during Ulysses' absence. The different characters enter separately or in small groups, and the introduction of each one further clarifies the situation. At the end of the first act Penélope summarizes the history of her life thus:

...all my life has been ravelling out... doing embroidery, dreaming... and waking up during the night, waking up from doing the embroidery and the dreams... ripping out. May the gods curse and destroy Helen! (p. 34)

In spite of however much the play may take one back to the Greeks, the work is not a tragedy because each one of the characters has the power to improve his situation but fails to use it. Although some external conflict takes place between the different characters, the most important action consists of the internal changes within Ulysses and Penélope.

During the war Ulysses apparently conducted himself with valor, or if he did not, there is no-one around to let the fact be known. When he returns home, he fears growing old, that he will no longer appear attractive to Penélope. He cannot or will not recognize this fear, becomes the victim of his passions, and kills his wife's suitors. If he had returned honestly, Penélope tells him, perhaps she would have found in him once again the man of her dreams. Instead, his pride leads to destruction.

Pride creates many of Penélope's problems, also, but with a different resolution. According to the classical inter-pretation of the *Odyssey*, Penélope represents virtue itself. Although she contemplates marriage because of her parents and suitors, her heart remains loyal to Ulysses. Buero points out, however, that even in the *Odyssey* she had her favorite suitor, Anfino, and that the *Odyssey* does not clarify the relationship between the two. Buero accentuates, instead of her virtue, her passions, her intelligence, and her sophistication. Penélope is every bit as astute as Ulysses, as is borne out in her handling of the suitors, but instead of possessing a cowardly, fearful pride like Ulysses, her's is jealous and possessive. She wants to be another Helen of Troy. The suitors make her feel young and desired. Perhaps she cannot cause a full scale war, but it delights her to think she is effecting a little skirmish.

Both Penélope and Ulysses appreciate Anfino's virtue and pureness while at the same time they realize it cannot survive for long in that practical world. After Anfino's death Ulysses decrees he shall be given a hero's funeral while the corpses of the other suitors will be dinner for the ravens. Ulysses admires the boy because he is not the coward the others are; he knows how to die. Penélope sees his kindness.

In the end Anfino's kindness inspires Penélope to reject Ulysses' cruelty. As Buero points out in his comments on the play, Ulysses won the exterior battle and lost the interior one. Penélope won the interior battle and lost the exterior.

In addition to differing from the Greek tragedies by focusing on personal moral problems, the play differs also in form by the inclusion of minor subplots, such as the triangle formed by Telémaco, Anfino, and Dione. Greek tragedy could relieve tension from time to time through the use of choral passages. Modern tragedy does it through this by-play. In addition, these incidents serve to clarify the action and further reveal the personalities involved. For example, in the case of the triangle just mentioned, Telémaco, Penélope's son, loves Dione, a slave, and she in turn loves Anfino, one of the suitors, who loves Penélope. Telémaco's carnal desires indicate he is little, if any, better than the suitors, for they too took the slaves to bed. He does not take Dione only because she will not go. Telémaco is his father's son, and his conduct suggests that probably in a similar situation Ulysses would have done the same. Telémaco and Ulysses could be considered as one man at two different stages of life.

The play contains several symbolic elements which should be mentioned, such as the Furies, Greek gods of the underworld who often returned to the world to avenge some wrong. In the play only the old nurse, Euriclea, hears them. She refers to them immediately before Telémaco enters followed by his father. Later she says she hears them just before the entrance of the four evil suitors. During the contest as Ulysses and Telémaco listen, she remarks that the Furies are listening. Towards the end of the play she cautions Ulysses to watch out for them.

The presence of the Furies suggests several things. Since Ulysses and his son kill the evil suitors, they may serve as the instrument of revenge or punishment chosen by the Furies. Aeschylus in the *Agamemnon* used evil to avenge evil and effect divine justice. Euriclea's cautioning of Ulysses at the end of the play indicates that while Ulysses may be the instrument of justice, he must also atone for his own sins. Her reference to the Furies before the entrance of the suitors further suggests that the suitors personify the Furies, forces of evil. These references may also indicate Euriclea's intuitiveness and awareness that each one carries within his breast Furies which may serve as instruments of vengeance or evil. This interpretation of the Furies parallels the idea of the beast within man developed more fully later in *Hoy es fiesta.*

The Greeks considered the Furies to be underworld gods. Except for the Furies, Buero's play contains only two references to the gods. The first occurs when Penélope prepares a sacrifice to the god of war and another to the god of love after announcing she will choose her husband by a contest. Buero does not elaborate on the results of this sacrifice. The other reference takes place at the end of the play as Penélope and Ulysses discuss their misfortunes.

ULYSSES: Everything is lost. The gods wanted to make our misfortune thus.
PENÉLOPE: Don't blame the gods. We ourselves brought it about.
ULYSSES: I'll leave... I'll pretend I have to fulfill a pledge of pilgrimage.
PENÉLOPE: Go, and continue pretending! (p. 84)

Buero does not talk of oracles or create miracles. His use of the gods seems undefined as he more or less puts them to one side and points out the moral corruption and personal responsibility of the individual.

Returning to the symbolic elements in the play, what about the war, or rather both wars, Helen's Trojan War and Penélope's little Trojan War? What do these wars mean, that took Ulysses from his hearth and caused Penélope to play with her suitors? Helen's war came about because Menelaus wanted to rescue his wife. Penélope says a woman capable of inciting such a war could not be contemplative or a dreamer, but rather must be like a contented animal. Ulysses claims she is so beautiful even the old men admire her and her husband forgives her infidelity.

I've seen her in Sparta... and I've understood the kidnapping and the crimes. I've felt, for the first time, ambitious for power and wealth in order to acquire that woman. (p. 20)

Then he concludes, perhaps diplomatically in order to quiet Penélope's fears, that Helen is nothing more than a bad and dangerous female. Does she represent only evil? Ulysses shows no remorse for having spent twenty years away from his home in her service, and undoubtedly he would go again. Helen and her war symbolize how men for lust and greed dissipate their energies in useless pursuits.

This war results in impoverishment of the palace. Feeling no guilt for her negligence, Penélope embroideries and dreams instead of tending to her husband's affairs.

I'm not the guilty one. If the Achaean armies bled for years, what does it matter if the flocks here lost a little blood? If we lose our husbands in their prime, and we see ourselves forced to remain on the home front only because one fool robbed another fool of some insignificant woman, who should be blamed for all the misery? (p. 32)

Wonderfully logical, her reasoning ignores the fact that the presence of the suitors represents military occupation of her country disguised as diplomatic courtesy. While she accepted them at first because they flattered her vanity, and she pretends they still do, underneath it all she is extremely frightened. She knows they could kill Anfino, her son, and even her. But rather than admit these fears, she takes flights of fantasy envisioning her war as not differing too greatly from Helen's. She attracts the sons rather than the fathers.

Thirty young chiefs, today old or dead, led our armies against Troy for Helen's sake. And thirty young chiefs, many of them sons of those before, came to compete for my sake! For me, for Penélope! Not for Helen, no! But for Penélope. It was my little revenge. My little Trojan War. (p. 45)

But what would have happened if she had tried to meet her suitors on some level other than that of frivolous flirtation?

Another symbol which should be mentioned is that of the blind nurse. In the *Odyssey* the nurse can see and she recognizes Ulysses by sight. In Buero's play she recognizes him by instinct. Of all the characters in the play, only she senses the presence of the Furies and the impending disaster. Once again Buero shows that at times the weak and humble possess great wisdom and foresight which could be used for the benefit of mankind, if mankind would permit it.

And finally, the play leaves the spectator with the question of values, the "life is a dream" theme. Anfino says to Ulysses,

You're killing me because you are already dead; remember what I'm telling you. Death is our great dream. To die in life is worse; I prefer to do it now. Thanks for your arrow, Ulysses. Death is our great liberating dream. (p. 76)

At the end of the play the chorus ironically sings of Penélope's virtue and loyalty while she, absorbed in Anfino's corpse, dreams of a day when there will be no more Helens or Ulysses in the world. "But for that we lack the universal word of love that only we the women dream... at times." (p. 86)

LA SEÑAL QUE SE ESPERA

T H I S play for me represents a concession by Buero to the demands of a Catholic society. He tries to please his public by talking about miracles in which he does not really believe in a manner which will not offend those who do. And his success from the dramatic point of view is questionable.

To begin with, he writes about people with whom he has no personal identity and with whom most likely he has not too much sympathy — talented middle-class professionals corrupted by their own egoisms until they have become victims of themselves, of their nerves, unable to contribute to society. But rather than attack their egoisms directly, Buero tries to understand them. At the end of the play I feel that while he may understand them, he nevertheless feels little compassion for their self-indulgence. The play exists as evidence to show how a totalitarian society can bring even an honest man to compromise himself.

The theme of nerves predominates throughout the play. Luis, a composer who cannot compose, is convalescing from a nervous breakdown at the home of the engineer

Enrique and his wife Susana. Susana comments about the boredom and nervousness of her husband. She herself takes tranquilizers. She tells Julian, the quiet, withdrawn philosophy professor, she hopes he will stay with them for a while, because it might help distract her husband. Julian had come to visit them because he too needed something to help him forget his problems. His wife had left him. The two servants exhibit their nervousness by annoying each other.

The plot revolves around an aeolian harp. Luis believes that if it will play a forgotten melody one afternoon, then he will again be able to compose. The two servants believe that when it plays they will receive a letter from their nephew, who had left many years previously in a fit of anger. Susana, because of her concern for the others, hopes also that it will play. Practical Enrique does not believe in silly superstitions, but humors them, for in his own desperation he too hopes for a miracle.

The miracle comes one afternoon when the nerves are at the breaking point. Enrique is jealous of Luis because he had been one of Susana's former boy friends, and he believes she still loves him. This, accompanied by financial problems, leads him to contemplate shooting himself. In his rage he orders an end to the nonsense of listening for the harp. His jealousy drives Susana to decide to throw herself in the sea. Then, for some unknown reason, instead of doing so, she returns to the house, goes to the harp, and plays the forgotten melody. At first the others accept the melody as a miracle, particularly since the servant's long awaited letter arrives the following day. Later they had been one of coincidence.

The main reason for these nerves lies in the fact that the individuals concerned could not accept the truth of their situation. When Susana rejected Luis and married Enrique, neither man could accept the truth. Luis told himself he had rejected her, and then hid from the truth even more in a nervous breakdown. Enrique likewise would not believe the truth of her love, but chose to believe she still loved Luis. One refused to accept an unpleasant truth, the other a pleasant one. In turn, Susana could not recognize her husband's jealousies and force him to break off his friendship with Luis. Julian, refusing to face up to the fact that he had to adapt to living with a younger woman, blamed his wife for their separation, her lack of adaptability to life with an older man. As in some of Buero's other plays, the characters can see but refuse to do so. This leads to a breakdown of communication. Truth remains a last resort, and all must fall to the bottom of the pit before recognizing their own egoisms. Still, none have committed a crime against society or done anything which would be socially unacceptable in most circles. Their moral corruption hides behind the mask of twentieth century respectability.

The playing of the aeolian harp taught these people the lessons of the miracle — work, love, pardon, and sorrow.

With the miracle a terrific urge to compose overwhelms Luis. Seeing himself as he is frees him from the mental block which prevented his working. Enrique learns he is bankrupt and will have to go to work. Julian prepares to return to his wife and work. Work becomes meaningful, purposeful, and gratifying.

They learn to trust each other and not let insincerity rob them of the fruits of love. Julian finds the courage to try to resolve his differences with his wife, and Enrique learns that Susana will stay with him through the misfortunes of life as well as the joys.

Also they learn to forgive. Julian's wife had abandoned him, but he comes to realize that part of the fault is his. While he must forgive her, she must also forgive him. Enrique, Susana, and Luis become aware of the suffering they have caused one another, and that all must be forgiven and forgotten.

Finally, the greatest lesson of all — they learn that the sorrows of life cannot be escaped. One cannot escape rejected love with a nervous breakdown, work by pretending to be rich, or a broken marriage by visiting friends. At times man must resign himself to suffer.

But what of the miracle, or sign? Are miracles of supernatural origin, or are they merely miracles of coincidence, as indicated here? Julian, the quiet philosophy professor, may be expressing the author's views on these questions:

I was thinking of how full the world is of coincidences. Of how we're all waiting for something. You see, I came here to wait, too... something else. Although I don't need signs, because for me everything is a sign. Especially, the sign you're waiting for. (p. 21)

In the world everything is a sign, my friend. Fate does not exist. (p. 21)

...everything is a miracle. Just the simple existence of things. The plant that grows is a miracle, although it doesn't give unusual flowers, and the harp, and the grotto of the voices, even though

we may think we know why they sound... A miracle is the
conception of a son, his birth, and his becoming a man. (p. 27)

Faith never is useless, Enrique... Faith moves mountains and
produces signs. We live by its power. (p. 57)

ENRIQUE: ...everything has been a miracle. A great miracle.
LUIS: No Enrique... My song was played by human hands.
JULIAN: And the letters were brought by human hands, and
            everything is human in this lowly world. And you're
            both right. Because everything is, also, marvelous.
            (p. 68)

In spite of the implications of these remarks, the work
still leaves some unanswered questions with respect to
modern miracles. The harp was played by human hands
and the letter the servants awaited was brought by human
hands, but the servants had believed it would come the
day the harp played. Was this a mere coincidence, or
was it a miracle? Would the letter have come if they
had not believed, would it have been a miracle which
they were unable to see — to which they were blind? Julian
received a letter the same day. Was his letter a miracle
also, although he had not believed? A few days previously
Enrique had received a letter telling him he was bankrupt.
In the end this bad news brings him true happiness, for
when he tells Susana, she tells him she will stay with
him. Are misfortunes sometimes miracles, also? Or is
everything merely coincidence?

With respect to the question about why things happen,
Buero has said that whereas in the past men though of
events as being the result of cause and effect, now intellectuals conceive events as the result of relationships.
The actual cause of an event may not be a direct cause,

and actually we know very little about why things happen. Applying these comments to the play, one could say that it is not as much an expression of what man knows about why things happen, as about what he does not know.

At the end of the play the orchestra begins to play softly, increasing in intensity until the end of the scene. The audience can hear the miraculous, powerful music. Those on the stage sense it, but hear nothing. Three times in his dramatic work Buero has used music to complete what he has to say — here, at the end of *Concierto,* and in *Tejedora* as Penelope sits weaving. This use of music indicates the author's recognition of the limitations of language and implies that the ultimate harmonies are inexpressible in human terms. As Buero has said, when an author arrives at his final limitations, he must then seek another means of expression.

CASI UN CUENTO DE HADAS

ALTHOUGH this play did not have too much success before the public, I find it among my favorites because of the poetic quality of the plot and the skill with which the author explores the question of human personality. In commenting about the play, Buero has said, "More than just a sentimental question about beauty and ugliness, basically it deals with the general question which includes that, the essence of human personality. Or expressed in another way, the doubt about what we may essentially be in view of that which circumstantially we seem to be." (p. 76)

The play is an adaptation of the story by Perrault based on the old myth of "Beauty and the Beast." Buero develops the question of personality by revealing the changes in those of the most important characters.

Leticia, the protagonist, is beautiful, but everyone in the court considers her stupid. At the beginning of the play she sits in the corner and plays with a doll. Instead of being stupid, she possesses great sensitivity. Upon learning she can be attractive to men, she becomes a coquette. Riquet, the ugly prince suitor, tells her she suffers only from a lack of affection resulting in fear. He seems to prove his point when he treats her kindly and she becomes more clever. Later he returns home, and, left alone with the superficiality of the court, she reverts to her childish ways. Perhaps she is basically a very intelligent person, but because of a lack of intellectual stimulation prefers to live in the childhood world of fantasy rather than endure the stupidities of those about her. Or perhaps subconsciously the others envy her intelligence and beauty, and react by refusing to recognize the former.

When one feels uncomfortable in a situation, he can do three things — adapt, become resentful, or escape into the world of fantasy. Leticia chooses the latter. How does this affect her personality? Is she really the childish little girl of her dreams, or a potentially charming, talented, mature woman? How much choice does she have in the situation? Could she rise against her parents and demand something more worth while than the hunt and the games of the court? How much can anyone rebel against his environment?

As it turns out in the play, the very ugly Prince Riquet courts her. She falls in love with him, and for a while he appears handsome to her. Then love grows tired and she sees him once again as ugly. Which is the true Riquet, the handsome one she sees under the illusion of love, or the ugly one that exists both before and after the illusion? Why is it that when she is under the illusion of love she seems most clever? Is that only an illusion too?

Buero presents this conflict very clearly by having both
the ugly Riquet and the beautiful Riquet on the stage at
the same time talking to each other and trying to rationalize
the situation.

UGLY RIQUET: No. Nobody has made her stop dreaming.
                     It was her stupid female blood, unable
                     to resist the presence of a handsome,
                     empty admirer.

HANDSOME RIQUET: But I was handsome for her, too, and I
                     wasn't empty.

UGLY RIQUET: You were? Wasn't everything a hollow
                     illusion? Or perhaps a lie? A suble lie
                     crystallizing even when you didn't dream
                     anyone else could make love to her?

HANDSOME RIQUET: No. Her expression was honest. I was
                     attractive to her and she loved me.

UGLY RIQUET: And now she doesn't love me. Oh my
                     God! What are we like? What are we
                     really like? Each one sees us in his own
                     way. How do you see us? How do you
                     see me? What am I to you?

HANDSOME RIQUET: Handsome?

UGLY RIQUET: Horrible? (He moves his trembling hands
                     over his face.) You see me like you made
                     me. Horrible. The others always saw me
                     that way, and it's now that she's right.

HANDSOME RIQUET: Or maybe not? Your truth, my Lord, is
                     an infinite love for all things. She loved
                     me, and because of that, I was her ideal.
                     Who can conquer an ideal?

UGLY RIQUET: Armando. (Brief pause)

HANDSOME RIQUET: I won't give up. We'll meet. I'll fight
                     for her.

UGLY RIQUET: (Laughs painfully) Poor deluded fool!
                     I know I won't. (Looks for the first time

at his strange companion.) They've killed
you within me, my poor friend. (They
have approached each other. He puts his
hands on his companion's shoulder.) And
now I am alone. Forever. ... I'm alone
and I'm horrifying.

HANDSOME RIQUET: I'm horrifying.

UGLY RIQUET: We're waking up from the deceptive dream
of beauty. One has to deny it. (p. 59)

Later Buero ironically expresses the modern tendency
to evade unpleasant truths by means of a conversation
between the ugly Riquet and the handsome Armando, Leticia's other suitor.

ARMANDO: When you arrived I was praising the delicacy of
our age. We've substituted the lighter rapiers of the
court for the heavy swords of our grandfathers;
and in love, uncouth ancient customs with urbanity.
No jealousy, abduction, or violence. The precious
flower of gallantry now flourishes in all Europe.
Isn't that right, girls?

IRENE: That's right, sir.

ARMANDO: (To Riquet) ... Our age is old and wise. It does
not believe in anything. Not even in those fiery
old passions which used to torment people... Tragedy is disappearing from our stages. The pastoral
is now in vogue.

ORIANA: I wouldn't say that, sir. Tragedy is always ready
to leap to the stage.

ARMANDO: (Smiling) Don't you believe it. Now we resolve
everything... playing.

ORIANA: But, as in that credulous age, sir, our games are
charged with passion when a woman is involved.

ARMANDO: And even if it were so, ma'am, we've invented the
most beautiful solution, which is to hide it. We've
invented education. Isn't that right, Prince?

RIQUET: Without a doubt, sir.
ARMANDO: Education, which is based on the substitution of
            words. If a coward, for example, is afraid to fight
            for the woman they've snatched from him, it's more
            courteous to call his cowardice sophistication. Isn't
            that how it sems to you, Prince? (p. 63)

In the end Leticia marries the ugly Riquet, accepting
with resignation the fact that in the future they will have
to bear the sorrows of life as well as the sorrows of his
ugliness. Buero could have had her marry the handsome
one, and then we would have had a Hollywood type ending,
but he knew that in so doing she would have been
marrying an illusion. If she married facing reality, her
love would grow and mature with the years instead of
withering and dying as she became aware of how difficult
a job it is to live. This ending also reflects the Spanish
point of view that marriage is a doubtful beginning, in
contrast with the American idea of a happy ending.

But was the beautiful Riquet really an illusion? Is love
blind? Or is love a kind of respect and understanding that
develops through the years as individuals share their joys
and sorrows? The answers as implied here seem to be the
same as in *Ardiente* — human love is no more than egoism.

Although Buero does not present any magic formula
for creating beauty and intelligence in Riquet and Leticia,
through Oriana, the human witch, he does suggest how
one can acquire an inner beauty which will in time reflect
itself in a softening of physical features.

As a young girl Oriana was very ugly, but she studied,
practiced self-discipline, and learned to have compassion
for others. By the time she was an old lady her features

had softened making her attractive. Although her ugliness had denied her children in her youth, in her old age she felt that all were her children. Was that an illusion? Can one who has never known the intimate love of a husband and children develop a heart large enough to include all as her children?

Although Oriana herself made the final decision to put her life to a constructive purpose rather than to hide it in bitterness, she was first of all encouraged to study by a doctor friend. Without his encouragment she might never have done it. Perhaps he contributed more to the development of her personality than she may have realized. When she decided to study and improve herself spiritually, did she not perhaps dream she could make herself beautiful through her works? Does anyone ever do anything except to gain a feeling of personal satisfaction? How would this dream have been different from that of Leticia's of a beautiful Riquet? Oriana became beautiful as she gave of herself. Riquet gave of himself to Leticia. Why didn't his beauty last, too, instead of remaining the illusion of her first love? What would Riquet have been like if he had been handsome? If he had been handsome, how much of his personality would have been determined by the more favorable treatment he would have received from those about him? Do we determine our personality, or is it only a reaction to the environment?

In considering these questions sooner or later one arrives at the tragic concept of necessity and personal liberty. A human being enters the world with certain physical assets and liabilities which will determine in part how his life will be. They may limit his activities and they certainly will influence how others respond to him. Like the ugly Oriana, they may deny him the joys of a family. However, the possibility remains that perhaps through study, self-discipline, and compassion he may acquire an inner beauty which may provide some compensating satisfactions.

Buero considers these same questions in *Concierto* with the emphasis shifting to the effect a lack of freedom may have on the development of human personality. Valindin cares for the beggars who play their violins for him. They receive their bread every day, have a place to stay at night, are clothed, and if they got sick, they would probably receive the needed medical attention because it is financially to Valindin's benefit to provide these things. But in having to depend upon him for everything, they lose their sense of dignity. They do not mind if people laugh at them and think them fools. Jealousies arise amongst them to the point that the boy Donato betrays his best friend, David, and David murders Valindin because he cannot lose himself into the homogeny of the masses.

Although an external autocratic force oppresses Leticia and the blind beggars, the same problems exist in the most modern, progressive, and democratic of societies. Increasing socialism, automation, the shorter work week, and increased hours of leisure all create problems in personality development. In both the case of the blind beggars and modern industry the individual must find meaning in his work. A worker may become one of the machines, or he may try to find some way to maintain his individual personality. If he cannot funnel his passions and energies into gratifying activities, he may release them like Donato and David in acts of violence, or like Leticia, he may escape into a world of fantasy.

At times in other plays personalities do not develop, not because of the external situation, but because of conditions within the individuals themselves. For example, in *Cartas* the members of the family instead of dealing frankly with one another enslave themselves to petty jealousies and resentments. In *Madrugada* the characters behave similarly and deny themselves the satisfactions of pleasant family relationships. In *Tejedora* Penélope hides her hopes and fears from others because she fears their cruelty. So it goes in one form or another with these characters each wearing a mask and hiding, or perhaps revealing, his true fearful self from the others.

Finally, is the question of human personality of great importance? Does it really matter if the individual loses himself in the mob or becomes another machine? Stricter law enforcement could perhaps reduce crime, at least among the masses, and more social activities might relieve nervous tensions. Looking to the plays for an answer, we find that in *Historia* the characters more or less conform and nothing is accomplished; in *Cartas* they become bitter and destroy themselves; in *Aventura* Silvano refuses to adapt and exposes the dictator Goldmann; in *Soñador* Esquilache yields to the demands of the people while remaining loyal to his higher personal ideals, and in so doing prevents a civil war; in *Ardiente* Ignacio refuses to conform and creates in Carlos an inner desire to learn profounder truths; Penélope in *Tejedora* rejects Ulysses' cruelty and finds her spiritual salvation; in *Señal* the characters can not create until they discover their individual weaknesses and individuality.

So while Buero does not tell us what human personality is, he illustrates its complexity and how it can be molded by the physical traits with which one is born, the mental attitude of the individual, and the society in which he lives. In addition, he shows the interaction of these factors upon each other. But the question remains, that of "what we may essentially be in view of that which circumstantially we may seem to be."

MADRUGADA

T H E ancient theme of love conquering death reappears once again in *Madrugada,* but instead of the usual sugary treatment, only stark realism shows how love may provide the physical strength necessary to confront life's greatest crisis. The action begins where it usually ends in a play of this theme — immediately after the death of Mauricio, the only successful member of the family. Thus from the very beginning the play shows things may not be what they seem. Death's greatest tragic effect may lie not with the deceased, perhaps, but rather among those left behind. The play takes place just before dawn employing only one hour and forty-five minutes, with the personalities of the characters providing the dramatic intensity. One by one the author removes their masks and discloses the motives of their lives — their individual tragedies.

Although this play was a hit with the public and is extremely well written, it is the one I like least of all. Here Buero tries to do something extremely difficult, if not impossible — to show the power of love while suggesting that true love differs from conventional concepts. He tries to stretch the limits of artistic expression to express the inexpressible — the abstraction of true love. I do not feel he completely succeeds.

The play begins shortly after the death of the painter Mauricio. Prior to his death he had lived for some time with Amalia, his model, marrying her unbeknownst to his family six months previously. During these six months Mauricio, a naturally quiet, reserved man, seemed unusually reserved and cold towards his wife. She did not understand why. She wondered why he had married her and why he had not remembered two members of his family in his will. Hoping she can trick his relatives into answering these questions, she summons them to the house, tells them Mauricio is dying, and that if they will disclose their conversations with him during the previous six months, she will not arouse him to sign his will. This will, she says, would leave his estate to her instead of them. Finally she learns Mauricio married her because he loved her, and he disinherited his brother and nephew because they had insulted her.

The author reveals almost all the details of the play during the first few minutes with the exception of why Mauricio had married Amalia and the identity of those who had spoken badly of her. The rest of the play consists for the most part of the psychological portrayal of the characters.

The resolution at the end arrives principally as the result of jealousy. Paula, Leandro's girl friend, followed him to the house. She suspects he is in love with Amalia and just playing around with her. This jealousy provides the double effect of at times giving Amalia sufficient courage to continue the quest, and finally supplying the evidence to incriminate the brother and nephew.

The very simple construction of the play fails to become monotonous because of Buero's skill in maintaining dramatic interest and in introducing new elements in order to achieve the maximum dramatic effect. Such incidents as the howling of the dog, Lorenzo's falling asleep, and Amalia's fainting help keep the work moving.

Another example is the introduction of Paula. Amalia had not invited her. When all the others had arrived, Amalia had issued her ultimatum, and things seemed to have almost arrived at a standstill, Paula arrives. Nobody knows why she is there or what she has to do with the action of the play. The spectator does not fully realize her importance until towards the end, but she is essential to the development of the plot. She permits the introduction of evidence that could not be otherwise presented.

Although the play seems primarily a psychological drama, in its depths it concerns itself with some of the more complex social and transcendental problems confronting modern man. Material poverty plays an important role, and the spectator may see as much symbolic social protest in that as he cares to see. Furthermore, since Mauricio's relatives are also spiritually poor, one can ponder the relationship between spiritual and physical poverty.

As in many of Buero's plays, the morally strongest characters are socially the most insignificant. Mónica, the thin, timid-appearing teen-age niece is the only relative who feels sorrow and compassion. Amalia, a fallen woman in the eyes of the others, finds the strength to carry her game through to the end because she loves Mauricio. The symbolic minded might say that the conflict between Amalia and the relatives symbolizes the conflict between love and evil. Amalia, or love, wins the moral victory.

With respect to death, Mauricio and Amalia find each other in the death which separates them. Before Mauricio died he told Amalia,

It's late now for us to tell each other many things, my poor Amalia.... But perhaps from the other side of death I'll recover you... No, I've not lost you. But perhaps I'll recover you... from the other side. (p. 15)

After the ordeal of the hours before dawn following his death, Amalia learns that he had truly loved her. The first sunlit rays of the new day found this love fusing with her sorrow.

In conclusion, this play attempts in a very conventional way to turn everything upside down and show that things may not be what they seem. Family relationships do not necessarily bind people together; they may serve rather to separate them. Strength is not always found among the strong, but instead quite frequently among the weak. Social status and age do not determine an individual's moral character. Money does not by itself bring happiness or make one a better person. While death may be a tragedy, it may also effect spiritual improvement. Love is not synonymous with happiness or sorrow with unhappiness, but rather love and sorrow, happiness and unhappiness, may be interwined until they cannot be separated. Perhaps those who cannot feel sorrow cannot love. And finally, love may not conquer death, but rather death may be the means by which one comes to recognize love.

IRENE, O EL TESORO

PREOCCUPATION about the nature of reality, the
"life is a dream" theme, permeates a great deal of Buero's
work with one of the most interesting considerations found
in *Irene, o el tesoro*. In the play Irene seems to lose her
mind after the death of her husband and the loss of
her unborn child. The husband apparently died because his
father was too miserly to buy the necessary medicines. In
her escape from the reality of her father-in-law's cruelty,
she imagines that a little boy elf comes to amuse her.

The *Alfil* edition of the play includes some remarks
by Buero in which he explains that he wanted to create
questions in the mind of the spectator in addition to en-
tertaining him. He succeeded very well. Written in a
much more reflective, intellectual manner than the doubt-
ridden *Ardiente*, this play is perhaps the most paradoxical
of all. Everything, from the title of the play and its
designation as a fable to the sanity of the characters, is
more or less contradictory.

In explaining the title, Buero asks if it means that
Irene is *el tesoro*, if it represents a choice by the elf
between *Irene* and *el tesoro*, or if it is just a simple title

113

expressed in two different ways. He calls the play a fable and wants the spectator to ask why. Is it a simple narration? Does it contain a moral? Or is it called a fable in order to emphasize the tragic tendency of the work? But rather than review Buero's comments about the complexities and paradoxes of the work, I will make my own observations with respect to some of the questions created about the nature of reality.

Although this play suggests many things, two questions seem fundamental, the first being, who is crazy? The play presents ample evidence to prove that Irene is crazy, that Dimas, her father-in-law is crazy, and that everybody is crazy. The spectator can take his choice.

Buero's definition of schizophrenia in the play by the Doctor Campoy proves Irene's insanity. He says that the schizophrenic hears voices, sees objects change color, and sees and talks with others. When Juanito, the elf, comes to visit Irene, he amuses her by showing her different colored lights. He talks with her and makes her laugh, but nobody else can see him. If nobody can see him but her, he must be an hallucination — a sure symptom of schizophrenia. But the Doctor decides Irene is not schizophrenic. She is merely unhappy and depressed because of her father-in-law's cruelty and the loss of her family. Placed in a more favorable environment, she would in time recover. If we accept this diagnosis, then the elf is no more than a figment of an overactive imagination.

On the other hand, the Doctor says greed has so consumed Dimas that he has become mentally unbalanced. The elf awakens him during the night by pounding upon the wall and pulling his nose. No-one else is awakened or hears the noise. If the elf is only a figment of Irene's imagination, perhaps Dimas really is so neurotic in his obsession for money that her imagination can suggest these hallucinations to him. That seems to be what the Doctor thinks. But at the same time, couldn't he just have nightmares, or a case of nerves? Although greedy, he seems to have sufficient control of his faculties to continue making and hoarding money. The world is full of people who like to hoard money, and very few of them are in insane asylums.

Then there is the possibility everybody is crazy, including the spectators. Buero expresses this idea beautifully. The lawyer Méndez is talking.

Perhaps we're all mad without realizing it. She goes mad because of the child she didn't have; he, for the money he craves all the time; Aurelia could go mad over a professor without a job or for a radio serial... Other women go mad because of trivialities... to go to the movies, to put on airs before the neighbors, to buy expensive stockings or silk handkerchiefs. And there are some who go mad in order to seek revenge. To get even with someone who deceived them although it may have been years ago; in order to return deceit for deceit, misfortune for misfortune. (p. 101)

Actually the decision about who is sane and who isn't depends to an extent upon answering the second question of the play: just exactly what do the elf and the Voice with which he converses represent? Nobody hears the Voice except the elf. The others do not even know it exists. We, the audience, hear it, so we can assume that in the mind of the author it exists, even though he does not tell us what it is.

The Voice had sent the elf to the house to seek a hidden treasure. In the end the Voice tells the elf that

the treasure is Irene and he must return with her. The
elf then leads her away on a marvelous road of light.
The others discover that she killed herself by falling from
the balcony.

The nature of the elf and the Voice can be explained
in three different ways. First, they may be purely biological
entities with the elf representing the imagination of Irene
arising from the subconscious, and the Voice representing
the lower levels of the subconscious of which one is unaware.
Psychologists have provided plenty of material to prove
that a great deal of activity goes on in the human subconscious which later comes to light as imagination. The
yearnings of the elf to know if he exists or not and the
implication that the Voice might represent God could be
no more than indications of the human desire to try to
rationalize his existence. The play substantiates this explanation in the scene where Dimas treats Irene cruelly and
she flees to the arms of Daniel — a purely instinctive act.
Nothing in the play seems to negate the possibility of
explaining the elf and the Voice as pure biology.

At the same time, this proposal is not conclusive
because it does not eliminate other possibilities. The elf
and the Voice could also represent a combination of the
subconscious and the Divine. Jung has suggested that
the lower regions of the subconscious may fuse with the
powers of the universe. This possibility is suggested in
the play when Juanito comments that he must be more
than a figment of Irene's imagination because he is more
clever than she. How could a person create something
better than himself?

A third possible explanation of the elf's presence is
that perhaps he came in response to Irene's prayers. He

first appears a few minutes after she prays for comfort to alleviate her terrible suffering. In that suffering she may have caught a glimpse of another world, a better world than the nightmarish dream world of human reality, and accidently walked off the balcony in a moment of preoccupation, or been led off, as Buero suggests. Each one of these explanations as to the existence of the elf and the Voice can stand by itself, but none eliminates the possibility that the others might not also be correct.

Although this is a play full of paradoxes and Buero has dedicated himself to making his spectator think, still, if one insists upon analyzing the work too closely, he will destroy much of its inherent beauty. A large portion of its merit lies in the fantastic quality of such things as the picturesque little elf and the beautiful colored lights which he shows Irene. These are poetic elements, and they cannot be placed upon a table and dissected. But until the public comes to realize that these inexplicable poetic elements are as valid as the rational, it is unlikely that works of this type will have much success before the public.

Hoy es fiesta presents a profounder, more detailed analysis of man's enslavement to poverty than that contained in *Historia*. The action takes place on a holiday as a group of neighbors meet on the roof top of a tenement to dry the laundry and enjoy the sun. The three different acts, as in *Historia*, show the passage of time, in this case, comprising only one day.

Prior to the day of the play, Doña Balbina, both spiritually and materially the poorest of all, but also the most pretentious, had sold fraudulent lottery tickets to her neighbors in order to obtain money to buy food. By chance the number of the false tickets wins and she is found out. Silverio, a man about fifty, persuades everyone to return the tickets and not press charges, but in the scuffle his wife is hit on the head. She dies at the end of the play. Ironically the one who loses most, Silverio, was the first to forgive.

Like *Historia,* the action begins on a very pleasant and somewhat humorous tone as the janitress, Nati, comes to hang up the laundry. Doña Nieves, a late riser still in her robe and with her hair uncombed, follows her. Then

two adolescent boys run out playing ball and stay to tease
Nati. Other neighbors enter wanting to enjoy the sun or
to hang out their clothes. The whole play emits the
atmosphere of working people on a day off, relaxing a
bit and catching up on miscellaneous chores. Nati, the
janitress tries to chase everyone away so she can lock
up the rooftop, but they refuse to go. Buero treats this
display of pride in the humble with sympathetic humor
and understanding.

The play contains very many characters, fifteen in fact,
but the author manages to create an intimacy with almost
all. The audience feels genuine compassion for the super-
stitious fortune teller, the youthful student afraid to do
anything which might damage his career, the ordinary
housewife bullied by her husband, the elderly man who
escapes into his magazines and his memories, and all the
rest. In the scene which best ties everybody together, each
one tells what he would do with the money if his ticket
would win in the lottery. Money to the poor represents
salvation. All share in its dream.

With the possible exception of the young student, these
people are not well educated. Most are extremely super-
stitious and pay out their hard-earned money to have their
fortunes read in the cards. Still, the fortuneteller does not
intentionally deceive them. Just a simple, stupid old woman
trying to make a living, she believes in the cards as much
as they do.

The sets and language in this play contribute much
to the dramatic effect achieved. The spectator sees the
dilapidated furniture, the rooftops with a few flower pots
set around to accent their austerity, the sooty chimneys —
everything very old and worn. Changes in the lighting

indicate the passing of the day, and the play ends as falling night and a darkening sky augment the feeling that this has indeed been a strange holiday. The crude language further contributes to the atmosphere of ignorance and poverty.

One of the greatest burdens the poor must confront is the monotony of life. Each day only repeats the previous one with an occasional holiday to break the routine. Or, turning the sentence around, anything that breaks the monotony, even if it is unpleasant, is a holiday.

Of course there is more than one way to react to this monotony. The play offers resignation as a solution. The characters resign themselves to their situation, to the impossibility of escaping from the bonds of poverty, and to the improbability of ever doing anything really worth while. The play also suggests that this is not the only solution. Perhaps one needs to dream loftier dreams. Silverio advises Fidel, the student, to forget his crazy ideals and content himself with realizable ambitions. Then he wonders if he had counseled correctly. Is it better to establish practical, realistic, realizable goals and end up on a tenement roof top, or is it better to set the goals higher and take a chance? Life has a way of changing everything anyway, so why not let it change an extravagant dream rather than a miserly one. If Silverio had exerted himself to develop his talents instead of accepting the realizable of the moment, perhaps he could have invented a hearing aid for his wife. One of his neighbors suggests this possibility. Perhaps in her stupidity and insensitivity she is expressing one of the greatest truths of the play. Buero likes to put some of his profoundest thoughts in the mouths of the most unlikely characters.

Hopes and dreams lead one to look to the future, but here Buero plays with time to fuse the past, the present, and the future until time loses all meaning in human existence, while at the same time, in this one day he depicts the whole human tragic situation from birth to death. Again, the paradox of Buero's work. Time has no meaning, but while saying that he defines life in terms of time.

Elías, Silverio, and Daniela represent the fusion of the past, the present, and the future. Elías, some fifty years old, lives in the past looking at old magazines. In his youth he worked for a publishing house, and in these old magazines he hopes to run across references to things he helped publish. He tells his friend Silverio

Man lives by hope, Silverio. And I too, although you don't believe it. I look at old magazines... But perhaps I do so in order to see in them some reflexion of a better future. (pp. 54-55)

Silverio lives in the present. In his youth he had shown great promise in several different fields of endeavor, but he had not developed his talents. Before he met Pilar, who later became his wife, she had been raped by an enemy soldier. Later she gave birth to a little girl. Although Silverio married her, he was extremely jealous of the child. One day he went to the country to paint, taking her with him. While he was carelessly absorbed in his painting, she was killed. The emotional shock of the child's death caused his wife to lose her hearing, and the incident left him with an inescapable feeling of guilt. Secretly he hoped that one day he would be brave enough to tell her that the child died because of his negligence, and that she would forgive him. But rather than face up to that future and her possible denial of forgiveness, he preferred to live day by day doing only the immediate tasks demanded of him.

Daniela, the young daughter of Doña Balbina, looks to the future. Her mother feels herself too good for local society, although she has less money than the others. Rather than let Daniela take a well paying job, she makes her sew in secret to earn money for the two of them. When the larder is completely bare, they dress up in their best clothes and crash a party somewhere. Of course they are sometimes discovered and thrown out, but that is part of the game. Daniela would like to escape from this life of lies and marry Fidel, the young student, but Fidel has pretentions also. He does not know she is even alive. Although young, she is stronger than either her mother or Fidel. She will have the responsibility of looking to the future and caring for others. Buero frequently places the heaviest responsibilities on the young or the weak. True strength lies in moral fiber, and this is no respecter of physical strength, wealth, or social position.

While each one of the three, Elías, Silverio, and Daniela, look with hope in a different direction, basically the situation with each one is the same. They are no more than three of the poor. The past, the present, and the future in themselves have no meaning.

Nevertheless, time moves on. Silverio's sorrow is the most personal one presented. As has been mentioned, guilt feelings plague him because of his jealousies and his negligence of his wife's child. Buero places a great deal of emphasis upon the conception of the child as the result of rape. In this rape one can see an implication about original sin, the suffering of the innocent, or perhaps about the rape of Spain during the Civil War. At the same time, it also suggests that a great deal of human suffering could be eliminated if human beings were only able to love another.

In depicting the relationship between Silverio and his wife's child, Buero shows how an individual develops not as an homogenous organism, but as a duality. Each one, even the most virtuous, has moments when the beast comes out in spite of whatever he may do. Silverio explains it thus:

Everything in life is so dark and mysterious... And we men are so small... Perhaps each one has only one day, or a few days, of clairvoyance and kindness.... But there are days... in which the worst comes out in all of us, the most brutal and unconfessable things. Days when we become another person... A hateful person that we were carrying within ourselves without knowing it. And we ourselves are that person... (p. 53)

Silverio himself possessed sufficient moral character to persuade the others to forgive Doña Balbina for selling them the false lottery tickets, but he had given vent to his jealousies against a defenseless, innocent child.

Silverio looked for a sign to indicate some hope for forgiveness. When he was able to prevent the neighbors from reporting Doña Balbina to the police and he was able to counsel her daughter Daniela, he felt he had had that sign, that then he could confess his guilt to his wife and she would forgive him. She died before he could tell her. Death requires the profoundest of human hopes, hope in that mysterious unknown, and hope for forgiveness for all human errors.

SILVERIO: Alone. I'm talking to you. To you, mysterious witness that we sometimes call conscience. And to you,
almost unnamable, to whom men talk when they
are alone without understanding to whom they're
speaking... Does this strange holiday have some
meaning? Should I understand it as a day of hope
and pardon? Through Daniela have I perhaps re-
deemed that poor child's life? But I know very well
you can only answer me through human lips. I know
that and I accept it. Because I loved only myself,
I destroyed my life. Although it's late, I should rebuild it. I've been perverse, and then a coward. I'll
change my ways. I know the day hasn't ended yet
for me, and that the most difficult test still lies
ahead. Help me to face it. (pp. 94-95)

Life then is a strange holiday, beginning with the human
being born to misfortune, but greeting it in his youth
with all the eagerness and freshness of the early morning.
Life brings with it sorrow, and ends as the day draws to
a close, in darkness and hope.

One has to hope... to always hope... Hope never ends... Hope
is infinite. (p. 96)

LAS CARTAS BOCA ABAJO

T H I S play, with the exception of the increased emphasis on guilt and some interesting symbolism, presents nothing new that has not been expressed previously in either *Historia* or *Fiesta*. Also like these earlier plays, this one contains very little action, concerning itself only with the tensions within the family as Juan, a man of about forty-five, takes the examinations for a position with the University. His son asks permission of his parents to accept a scholarship for study abroad. At the end of the play his father grants him permission to go and announces to the family that he has failed the examinations.

Actually the story began many years prior to the incidents depicted on the stage. When Juan's wife, Adela, was about ten, her mother died. After that her sister Anita assumed the responsibilities of a mother caring for Adela and her brother Mauro. Later Anita fell in love with Carlos Ferrer, but Adela broke up the romance by making a play for him. When Carlos lost interest in Adela, she married Juan, determined to make a great success of him in order to spite Carlos. Anita, full of bitterness and resentment because of the broken romance, came to live with Juan and Adela, but never speaks to them. Then the situation becomes reversed. Instead of Anita being the head of the household with Adela the little girl, Adela is the head of the household with Anita the little girl.

Anita haunts Adela like her conscience. Juan never fully understands the conflict between the two women, but he understands enough to resent Carlos Ferrer. Also, he resents Carlos' professional succes and refuses to read his books or to recognize that his work has merit. He fails to pass the examinations because he would not familiarize himself with Ferrer's work.

Frequent visits by Mauro, Adela's brother, further complicate the family situation. He imposes upon their hospitality, but Adela permits him to come because he brings word of Carlos, whom she imagines as a secret lover.

Juan, Anita, and Adela love Juanito, the son, but they use him as an instrument to hurt one another. The family stays together bound by mutual hatreds and antagonism rather than by love and understanding.

The intertwining of the lives of Adela, Anita, and Juan, and their inability to communicate is most graphically depicted in two very similar scenes. In one Adela begs Anita to forgive her and to talk to her. Anita refuses. In another scene Juan begs Adela to talk to him, not to treat him with indifference. He wants her to turn her cards face up. She refuses. Her refusal leads him to trick her in order to find out what her feelings really are. After failing the examination, he tells her that he has passed. She does not respond with much enthusiasm. When the boy comes in a few minutes later and tells his father he is sorry he failed, then Adela appears pleased.

This simple play contains some very interesting examples of symbolism. As Mauro indicates, Anita's silence represents Adela's conscience. She can never free herself from this silent disapproval. And while Anita exerts pressure upon Adela, Adela likewise exerts pressure upon her husband, constantly reminding him of his failures.

Anita's inability to talk resulted from a psychological rather than a physical handicap. Perhaps because of the responsibilities and shock of her mother's death and her broken romance, for a while her emotional state was such that she actually could not talk. But rather than overcome this defect and escape from her muteness, she withdrew into herself and let it become a permanent habit. In a touching scene before Juan's final exam she wants to wish him luck, and having just completed the jersey she has been knitting, she gives it to him to show her affection. But no matter how much she may want to talk, the words do not come out.

No such physical limitation exists between Juan and Adela. They talk to each other all the time, but they do not communicate. Like the mute Anita, they have made themselves victims of their habits—their unwillingness to show their cards face up. All of them have created for themselves a human limitation where none need exist.

Carlos Ferrer Díaz continues this idea of the human creation of limitations. He never appears in the play and we have no idea how he looks. We know only that about eighteen years previously he was Anita's beau and then Adela's. Through the years he has become a successful author. No actual contact exists between him and the family, but he does more to shape the conduct and personalities of his group than any one of them. He lives like a ghost in the house. Juan is too proud to read his books. The son Juanito imagines he is a better man than his father because he has had greater material success. Anita cannot forget that Adela broke up her courtship. And Adela dreams that Carlos must still be in love with her. By the inclusion of this character the audience never sees and in one sense does not even exist, Buero further symbolizes how hatreds and resentments can be imagined.

Carlos Ferrer Díaz can also be interpreted as the "good life." Each one of the characters sees in him some material quality lacking in his own life. Ferrer represents a better, an ideal situation. But he has probably forgotten he ever knew them. The "good life" is a myth, an illusion, a figment of the imagination, a purely material condition.

Another example of symbolism in this play lies in Mauro, Anita and Adela's brother. He is lazy, shameless, cynical—the picaro of the twentieth century. In his youth he enjoyed life, but through the years he became bored with everything. Although a failure, he feels no shame because he knows he does not differ from many others who appear to have been more successful but have also failed. Everything about this man is little and miserly, from dreaming miserly dreams to committing petty crimes. He tells his nephew Juan, "Someday, I know, they'll take me to jail for taking a few dollars... And you will continue greeting people who have robbed millions." (p. 60)

Because of his pettiness, Mauro tries to please everybody by telling them just what they want to hear; the truth carries very little weight. He portrays himself like this:

I look inside myself and I don't even find repugnance because I'm empty. I've been for you what I've been for all: a mirror that returns your reflection. (p. 84)

Although empty, he is still the philosopher of the play:

MAURO: A while back I leafed through an interesting little book. You'd like to read it. It said the birds sing happily in the morning because the sun comes out and a pleasant day's journey awaits them which they expect to be full of delightful adventures. They're like us during the morning of our life: astounded. But during the afternoon they don't sing.

ADELA: Don't you hear them?

MAURO: Those aren't songs: they're shrieks.

ADELA: What are you saying?

MAURO: They're shrieking from terror. All that which seems to you a delirium of happiness is a delirium of fear... At the end of the day they've had time to remember that they're beneath the hard law of fear and death. And the sun goes away, and they doubt that it will return. And then they search and go mad and they try to be astounded... But they don't succeed. They want to sing but only shrieks come out. (pp. 85-86)

Fiesta expressed this same idea.

The world is full of people like Mauro. They have read books and can repeat the pretty things they have found in them. They adapt to the demands of their environment, are well-adjusted, and reflect perfectly what their companions want to see. They are even "popular." But they are empty. Nothing comes from within them. If anything did, it would run headlong into the conformity of their environment. This type is the exact opposite of the rebels we find in Buero's work. The rebels have faith in themselves to the extent that at least they are not afraid at times to oppose the old, corrupt, and useless. The mirrors, like Mauro, have faith in nothing.

Whatever honesty there is within the individuals participating in this drama prior to the final moments of the play is found in Juanito, the son. He typifies a certain type of young person frequently found in Buero's work. In *Cartas,* as in *Historia,* the older generation seems tired, discouraged, and corrupt in contrast to the freshness and youth of the younger. And like the young people in *Historia* and *Fiesta,* as Juanito comes to be ashamed of his parent's conduct, he at the same time discovers he loves them. Fernando in *Historia* provided for his mother; Daniela in *Fiesta* loved her mother so much she considered committing suicide rather than face the humiliation which would follow exposing her. Juanito here expresses genuine sympathy for his father's failure and offers to stay with the family instead of accepting the scholarship. In one sense these young people reflect the filial affection and respect common to the Spanish culture, while at the same time they do not feel completely comfortable with their inheritance from the past. This generation may contain a latent rebellion suppressed by a lack of personal freedom.

The conclusion of the play is typically Buero, with the adults coming to recognize their weaknesses and acknowledging their failures as the young son goes out into the world to blaze a new way.

In spite of the prosaic plot, this play was well received by the public, probably because of Buero's skill in creating live personalities with whom his spectators can readily identify.

UN SOÑADOR PARA UN PUEBLO

Un soñador para un pueblo is a landmark in Buero's dramatic career for several reasons. First, it marks the beginning of a new dramatic style which he uses later in the other two works included in the historical trilogy —*Concierto* and *Las Meninas*. In these three plays he tries to analyze contemporary problems not by looking at the daily lives of his characters, or by fleeing into the world of myth, but instead by seeking their roots in history. In the eighteenth century world of *Soñador*, for example, Spain had an opportunity to enter the world of modern European nations, but frightened by the cruelties of the French Revolution, she backed off. Now in the second half of the twentieth century she has another opportunity, and Buero asks, will she back off again?

In addition to looking to history for the sources of the problems, these historical plays also show a change in Buero's dramatic technique. He loads the stage with characters, colorful costumes, elaborate and numerous scene changes. These plays are all extravagant productions.

Looking at *Soñador* more closely from a contemporary viewpoint, the play marks Buero's most critical analysis of political and religious problems. It is based upon the riots of 1766 during the reign of Carlos III in protest against the King's minister, Esquilache. History tells us that when Carlos III became king, he brought Esquilache with him from Italy to replace Ensenada as minister. Esquilache effected many reforms which the conservatives of the time opposed. His proclamation prohibiting the wearing of long capes and broad brimmed slouch hats in order to reduce crime in the city triggered the revolt. An uprising and a riot took place the following Palm Sunday. The leaders of the revolt made several demands upon the King, including the removal of Esquilache, not only for his reforms, but because he was an Italian. After meeting with his ministers, the King decided to cede to the demands of the people. Esquilache then left the country in exile. This is according to history. [1]

The play centers about this event with the only deviation by Buero occurring near the end when he changes events slightly so as to have Esquilache make the decision to leave the country and prevent a civil war. In addition to remaining loyal to the data, Buero develops clearly and in detail the atmosphere of the time by including such particulars as Esquilache's address, current religious atti-

---

[1] Volumes 1 and 2 of *Historia del reinado de Carlos III en España* by D. Antonio Ferrer del Río (Madrid, 1856) contains a fairly detailed description of these events. In *Insula* ("Tres preguntas a Buero Vallejo," 147, febrero, 1959, p. 4) Buero listed his sources of information as Feijoo, Torres Villarroel, Don Ramón de la Cruz, *La vida de Carlos III* by Fernán Núñez, *Historia del reinado de Carlos III* by Danvila y Callado, Ferrer del Río, Marañón, Fernando Díaz-Plaja, Sáinz de Robles, and *L'Espagne éclairée* by Sarrailh.

tudes, the improvements effected by Esquilache, and char-arters taken from and representative of that century. In addition, the character portrayal contributes to the universal qualities of the work.

Buero's Esquilache, for example, is a universal character belonging to all time. Getting along in years, he is tired and finds pleasure in such simple things as a cup of hot chocolate. At the same time, a shrewd, ambitious politician, he is on his toes every minute in order to keep ahead of his enemies. His practicality fuses with an idealism which dreams of a better Spain, with the latter leading him to install street lights, promote crime prevention, build roads, improve sanitation facilities, and many other civic improvements. In the end the people revolt against him. How does he differ from a modern business man who faces constant competition in order to maintain his professional or economic position, tired and anxious to relax in the evening a bit before his dinner, and who dreams of a better education for his children and civic improvements for his city?

Esquilache's wife likewise lives in the 18th century but is like many women of today, bored with staying home alone all day while her husband works. She has ambitions for her children and uses her influence to help them get ahead. The social life of the court attracts her, and in her solitude at times she seeks male companionship. Doesn't that sound like the 20th century?

On the other hand, King Carlos is a very different type of person. Both history and the play represent him as a gentle man, loved by his people, loyal to his deceased wife, a hunting fan, and dedicated to improving the lives of his subjects. His portrayal reflects an admiration on the author's part, an admiration which led him to name his first son in memory of this noble king. Likewise the other characters fulfill the dual roles of depicting history and representing contemporary personality traits.

The conflict in both the play and in history takes place between the conservatives who wish to retain the glory of the 17th century and the liberals who recognize that Spain cannot live in the past forever, but must adapt to new ways of doing things.

Since the days of the Catholic Kings the three strong political powers in Spain have been the church, the nobility, and the army. These three powers remain powerful in Spain today. The play depicts the conflict as it concerns the nobility and the church. The army today, of course, is controlled by Franco, and perhaps the fact that Buero does not include it in his considerations may indicate something about the social conditions in Spain at the time he wrote the play.

The cause of the uprising, according to Buero, lies with Ensenada, the minister prior to Esquilache. Both history and the play tell us that Ensenada tried to gain favor with Carlos III and regain a position in the government, but never succeeded. He was exiled shortly after the uprising. His actual role in the uprising is unknown today because many of the records have disappeared. There are a number of theories about the cause, and certainly Buero's is as valid as any of the others.

Others theories accuse the Jesuits and secrets groups of noblemen who wished to get rid of Esquilache and discourage further reforms. After the uprising a royal commission found the Jesuits guilty of using their influence to incite the riots. Carlos later expelled them from the

country. Books have been written maintaining both that
the Jesuits were responsible for the riots and that they
were not. Buero says he did not implicate them directly
because nothing had been proven against them. This is
very characteristic of this author. For him a man is always
innocent until proven guilty. However, since it is known
that Ensenada was very friendly with the Jesuits, the reader
or spectator can make his own speculations as to the influence they might have had.

In considering this aspect of the play, it is interesting
to recall that the Jesuits were expelled a second time
shortly before the beginning of the Spanish Civil War of
this century, and that Buero was thinking of the founder
of the Society of Jesus when he wrote *Ardiente*. Furthermore, it has been suggested that Carlos III does not receive more favorable comment in Spain today because of
his expulsion of the Jesuits.

Actually, whether the Jesuits had anything to do with
the uprising or not is of little importance as far as the
play is concerned. Rather, the question is that of the role
of the church in government and social improvements. No
country can escape this question. Germany and Russia have
tried unsuccessfully at different times to remove the church
from society. The United States supposedly has complete
separation of the church and state, but the courts have
one case after another in which they have to decide just
exactly what this means. Religion is a human need which
the individual expresses in a social context. In one form
or another the problem of the church and society, or the
church and the government will always be with us.

The play also raises the question of faith and fear.
Many people at the time of Carlos III feared the

destruction of the Catholic faith, and this contributed to their conservativism. Did they really want to preserve the faith, or was their own faith so weak they were afraid to confront it with new ideas? The play seems to indicate that if the Catholic faith is true, it cannot be destroyed. A conversation between Esquilache and Villasanta considers modernization of the church.

ESQUILACHE: There isn't a devouter man anywhere than King Carlos, and you know he wouldn't tolerate anyone near him that wasn't a fervent Catholic.

VILLASANTA: No doubt that's why you've put out the fires of the Inquisition.

ESQUILACHE: We've put out the fires of the Inquisition because we're good Christians. Modern times have shown us it's inhuman to burn someone alive, even if he's a heretic. The fire of hell is God's mystery, Duke; we don't burn it here on earth.

VILLASANTA: Words, words, Marquis. Words that hide your disbelief, and which will bring us the worst if we don't stop it in time.

ESQUILACHE: The worst?

VILLASANTA: The disappearance from Spain of our Holy Faith.

ESQUILACHE: You've little faith if you believe it can disappear so easily. I assure you that within one or two centuries even the most die-hard Catholics won't consider burning anyone alive for being a heretic. And religion won't disappear because of it. Perhaps those Catholics will believe they're following directly in your footsteps, but in reality, they'll be following us. And that's the whole secret: we're moving ahead and you and your kind don't want to move. But history does go on. (p. 43)

Applying this conversation to the current situation, one confronts not only the abstract question of faith and fear but also more concrete ones about such things as the ecumenical movement, birth control, and modernization of the church. While it is easy to see the error of burning people alive in the 18th century, it can be very difficult to evaluate and accept some of the new religious concepts of this century.

Another idea suggested here has to do with the relationship between society's social conscience and religious fervor. When religious zeal seemed at its peak, people were burned at the stake. Today when it is perhaps at an all time low, responsible citizens discuss the advisability of eliminating capital punishment and seek ways to avoid war. Government aid for the poor has replaced beggars on the streets. Man in his evolution is learning compassion. How does one explain this? Is man looking to himself now as a source of hope, as has been suggested by Sartre, Camus, and Buero, instead of accepting an irreversible destiny? If so, how far can he go?

Conservativism in the play does not confine itself to religion. In the 18th century it impeded social and industrial reforms. The people did not want to change their habits—to wear different clothing styles, to have fancy new street lights, to quit throwing their garbage in the streets. Today society is still making social and industrial reforms. Underdeveloped nations have trouble adapting to mechanization, and more advanced ones wonder how they can adjust to life with the computer.

In addition to these social and religious problems of conservativism and liberalism, the play also considers the conflicts between social classes and the responsibilities of government. The following scene between Esquilache, a foreigner, and Ensenada, a displaced nobleman, illustrates this.

ESQUILACHE: *(speaking of the King)* He arranged this meeting in order to give us a silent and formidable lesson.

ENSENADA: What lesson?

ESQUILACHE: He brings us face to face so we can compare ourselves. I compare myself with you and I understand.

ENSENADA: He what?

ESQUILACHE: You're right. I am worth less than you. And nevertheless, I'm greater than you. The most insignificant of men is greater than you if he lives for something besides himself. You haven't believed in anything for the past twenty years. And you're lost.

ENSENADA: And what can we believe in, we who work for the public? You can see there isn't any public. The tragedy of the one who governs is to find that out.

ESQUILACHE: A fine excuse for bad politics! But they could say the opposite: that their tragedy is to see how the greatest of politicians loses his ambition. (pp. 99-100)

Although no doubt Buero is thinking of his own people and the political situation in Spain, the problems are universal. In fact, his words may have an even greater meaning in democratic nations than for the people of Spain, for in a democracy the people have more opportunities to demand good government and more obligations as voting citizens. Is the individual voter who studies the issues and votes intelligently of greater worth than the corrupt politician? One thing seems sure; if enough individual voters act, the corrupt politician can be removed from office. And no-one asks the voter his social status.

Buero expresses the idea of individual responsibility most forcefully when he has Esquilache make the decision to accept exile according to the wishes of the people rather than risk a civil war. At this moment Esquilache sacrifices himself for the common good, thus representing the individual who persists in his desire for democracy during an age when it was extremely difficult to attain—persisting to the point of self-sacrifice.

Buero clarifies his own attitude and faith in democracy in the conservation between Esquilache and Fernandita, his servant girl, when Esquilache tells her that improvement "depends on you," "you" meaning the people, the servants, and others of lowly station.

ESQUILACHE: I believe in you, Fernandita. The people are not the hell you've seen! the people are you! It's in you, as it was in poor Julian and as it was in that man with the cloak yesterday, capable of having pity on an old man and a girl... They're hidden in your hearts! Perhaps centuries will pass before you understand. Perhaps your sad darkness will never be replaced by light. But it depends on you! Can you do it? (p. 104)

This faith in the people expressed here was written by a man living beneath a dictator and depending upon the whims of the public for his livelihood!

In this scene and the events that lead up to it Buero reveals his great understanding of democracy and how it works. Basically democracy is and always has been a radical idea. Many of the founding fathers of the United States had grave doubts about the advisability of placing the responsibilites of government in the hands of the uneducated masses. The same fear exists today, usually

hidden under the pretext of the Communistic menace. Democracy as an ideal asks the best of each member of
society—something that can never be obtained. And it
dreams of providing the individual with complete liberty
and all the fruits of a good life—something else that can
never be completely obtained. Because it is idealistic and
its errors are usually available for public inspection, in
practice it may appear far from Utopian. Buero realizes
all this, and so can write a plea for democracy that does
not promise to cure all ills.

Here in the play the people are for the most part uneducated and backward in their ways. Their conservative
leaders dupe them into staging a revolt. Some are killed
and the street lights which Esquilache had installed are
destroyed. The people must learn to govern themselves.
They will have to study and learn new and better ways
to do things. Corrupt leaders must be revealed and replaced. Improvements will have to come from within. Esquilache believes this, and, in his love for the masses,
leaves them to struggle forth in their own way, confident
they can do it.

This work has been misunderstood and is easy to mis-
understand because it is hard to believe such a strong plea
for democracy with such a profound understanding of
exactly what it involves could come out of dictatorial
Spain. Eric Fromm in *Escape from Freedom* has said that
only those who do not have freedom want it; those who
have it find its responsibilities terrifying. If so, Buero
seems an exception. He knows the problems that confront
a democratic nation and is ready to face them. When I
read this play and think of the anguish Buero must have
suffered when it was attacked by his enemies, misinter-

preted by his friends, and banned in two cities, I feel a
little ashamed that those of us who enjoy life in a democracy do not do more to extend its benefits to those
who do not.

WHICH is Buero's best play? Only the impartial judge of time can tell us that. *Historia* merits nomination because of the originality of conception and simplicity of construction; and *Ardiente* and *Concierto* because they express most forcefully the tragic concept. Buero himself feels these last two best express the essence of his work, and from the transcendental point of view, I would have to agree. However, for me *Las Meninas* is more representative of his work as a whole, for in this play one can find an example of almost every aspect of Buero's theatrical work—his weaknesses as well as his virtues. Like Velázquez, it seems like Buero tried to incorporate all he had learned about writing in this one artistic creation, *Las Meninas*.

The majority of the plays discussed heretofore have been characterized by precise, careful construction with little or no change of scene. In *Historia* all the action takes place on a stairway, in *Ardiente* in a school lounge, and even *Soñador* and *Concierto* do not have an excessive number of scene changes. In *Las Meninas* the scenes

142

change frequently from the balcony to the street to Velazquez' house, etc. In fact, they change so quickly the play
seems almost a movie. While this effect is spectacular, at
the same time I wonder if it does not represent a concession on the part of the author to conventionality.

In other plays the scenes have contained at times an
inherent artistic and aesthetic quality, such as the simplicity of the stairway in *Historia* and the colorful dream
scene in *Aventura*. Artistic qualities are as evident in this
play as in any, beginning with colorful costuming and
ending with a tableau at the end duplicating the painting
Las Meninas.

The play has a ficticious plot although the historical
setting is accurate. Velázquez is preparing to paint *Las
Meninas* after having just completed a nude study. His
enemies complain to the Inquisition about the nude; he
is called before the King; and the King asks him to destroy it. When he refuses, the King pardons him.

Some critics have claimed that Buero distorted history
and have attempted to point out historical errors in the
play, as for example falsification of the character Velázquez. I fail to see the justification of this criticism, although
some items, such as Velázquez' personality and his painting
of the nude are controversial. All the characters with the
exception of the two beggars actually lived.

The incidents, as usual in Buero's work, are very carefully selected with all pertaining directly to the author's
objective in relating his story and recreating the atmosphere of the period. For example, superstition, as portrayed in the scene at the end of the first part when two
ladies-in-waiting are looking for a ball of fire in the sky
as a sign that the Queen will give birth to a boy, and as

portrayed by Velázquez' wife's fears that the Devil possesses him, made up part of the world in which Velázquez
lived. Inclusion of this superstition, although incidental to
the plot, helps clarify Buero's purpose—to show the loneliness of a man of insight in that world of madness.

Buero's technique for character portrayal is the same
as in his other plays—to make them as true to life as
possible by portraying not only the historical data but the
universal qualities which make their lives meaningful to
all men.

The one exception from the historical standpoint, Buero
has pointed out, may be José Nieto, who may or may not
have been a member of the *Santo Oficio*. Historically
speaking it would have been possible, for anyone in good
standing with the church could be named a member. The
dwarfs and different palace personnel are all true to the
times.

Buero's attention to these small historical details is
further illustrated by the identification of Don Diego Ruiz
de Azcona in the painting. Buero says that Sánchez Cantón in his article "Las Meninas y sus personajes" published
in 1943 considered the identity of the *guardadamas* as
unknown. [1] The following year the Marquis de Saltillo in
an article entitled "En torno a Las Meninas y sus personajes" suggested it may have been Ruiz de Azcona. [2] He
based his conclusion on a will left by Doña Marcela de
Ulloa. Ruiz de Azcona also witnessed the will. Because
of this familiarity, Saltillo believed Ruiz de Azcona was

---

[1] Francisco Javier Sánchez Cantón, *Las Meninas y sus personajes*, Barcelona: Editorial Juventud, 1943.

[2] *Arte Español: Revista de la Sociedad Española de Amigos
del Arte*, cuarto trimestre de 1944.

probably the *guardadamas* in the painting. His conclusion seemed logical to Buero, so he used it in his play.

The other characters are just as carefully sketched. Doña Juana, Velázquez' wife, was a quiet, loyal helpmate who dedicated herself to her husband and children, and later to her grandchildren. Little is known of her other than that she was patient and long-suffering, the daughter of her husband's teacher, and that she died eight days after her husband. Apparently they were true to each other.

More is known about Princess María Teresa. A strong-willed girl in the play, she rebels against the loose morals of the castle and defends Valázquez against the attacks of his enemies. Buero suggests she was excluded from the royal family in the portrait *Las Meninas* because of this defiant attitude. Although the particular incident presented in the play probably never occurred, this reason never-theless remains a possibility.

José López Jiménez in *La vida y la obra de Velázquez* claims papers of that period indicate that her personal attitude was opposed to the manner in which public affairs were being handled. He quotes a letter: "They say that the oldest infante had a serious talk with her father during the past few days about what is going on, that she is full of spirit and stubbornness, and the King was greatly impressed by what he heard." [3] With respect to this, Buero has commented that this hypothesis about the exclusion of the Princess from the painting originated with Sánchez Cantón in the aforementioned work. He also notes that the letter was dated December 13, 1656, and therefore was

---

[3] Madrid: Compañía Bibliográfica Española, S. A., 1955, pp. 197-9.

probably written after the execution of the painting. If such were the case, it would be representative of what was probably the general attitude of the Princess rather than a particular incident.

The weak personality and moral stature of the King as portrayed by Buero are easily confirmed by almost any book on that period. In spite of this, the realistic portrayal of a weak king created a negative reaction among the monarchical elements within the country when the play was produced, as they interpreted it as criticism of them.

Some critics have maintained that Buero falsified the King's position and his relationship with Velázquez, and that may be. At the same time ample evidence exists to the contrary. The role of the Conde-Duque in the politics of the time bears out the King's weakness and that others manipulated his activities. Letters from the King ordering payment to Velázquez for his work that were never honored substantiate that member's of Felipe's court defied him. And that Velázquez himself defied the King is indicated by the fact that when he went to Italy the second time, the King repeatedly sent for him to come home. López Jiménez includes a letter from the King urging his return written sixteen months prior to Velázquez' actual departure from Italy.

That the painting *Las Meninas* was an act of defiance seems less certain. Critics of Velázquez complain in the play that he is showing disrespect in portraying the King and Queen reflected in a mirror at the back with the positions of importance in the picture given to a child, the dwarfs, and a dog. About 1620, 36 years previously, Velázquez made a picture somewhat similar — *Cristo en casa de Marta.* In the foreground Martha is preparing the meal and the very small figures of Christ and Mary are seen through the window. Mary is about the same size as one of the fish on Martha's table, and Christ is only slightly larger than the wine jug. In this picture Velázquez may not necessarily have been expressing disdain for the small figures. Instead, perhaps he felt compassion and understanding for Martha, who had been denied the insight of Mary; or perhaps he was only seeking a new perspective for an old story. *Las Meninas* could be no more than duplication of a form tried earlier. On the other hand, it could be a new perspective, and therefore a form of rebellion agains the old.

Guillermo Díaz-Plaja has written a very interesting article [4] about the picture in which he describes it as a picture with different centers of interest — technical, thematic, and psychological — which dispute among themselves the position of highest honor, and in so doing create among the characters a clamor for their right to independent existence. Likewise Buero's characters each clamor for an independent existence.

Returning to Velázquez and the King, history reports that the King was so fond of him that he defied his counselors in making him *aposentador mayor.* When the Order of Santiago refused to admit Velázquez because he could not prove his lack of Jewish or Moorish blood, the King wrote the Pope asking a special dispensation. All in all, the relationships between the three, Velázquez, María Teresa, and the King seem to be sufficiently complex

---

[4] "El secreto de 'Las Meninas'," *El Estilo de San Ignacio y Otras Páginas,* Barcelona: Editorial Noguer, S. A., 1956.

so that one cannot say whether their attitudes in the play have been exaggerated or not. Nobody knows what the relationships between them were. Perhaps at times María Teresa and Velázquez really did show the defiance and disrespect to the King that appear in the play.

Just what Velázquez was like is a still more difficult question. The sources consulted indicate that he was quiet, phlematic, dependable, cautious, reserved, and loyal. He had many other duties in addition to painting and actually was little more than a servant who painted. As *aposentador mayor*, his highest position, he had general charge of the palace. Buero indicates these extra duties in the play when Velázquez discusses with the Marquis the problem of paying the janitors. In addition to the honor of being *aposentador mayor*, two of his more important duties included redecorating the Alcázar and arranging the wedding preparations for María Teresa. I find it difficult to imagine him having been given such responsible positions if he had been excessively phlematic or too reticent in his dealings with others, particularly considering the intrigue existing within the court at that time.

The description of caution is also difficult to reconcile with his painting. Perhaps discrete would be a better word. He painted the first nude of a woman in the history of Spanish art. Goya is the only other early Spanish painter who dared paint a nude. Prior to Velázquez' time Spanish art had consisted almost entirely of religious pieces and portraits. Velázquez painted many portraits but relatively few religious pieces. While Spanish painting at that time was little more than another vehicle for singing the glories of religion, in Italy painters enjoyed the themes of mythology, the nude, and the beauty and harmony of the body. Painters there were engrossed in a profound realism. Velázquez is noted for his realism, but it is a visual realism, one depicting what the eye actually sees. His realism was controversial at the time, and critics still discuss it. More than likely he tarried in Italy on his second trip because of the artistic stimulation which he received from the other painters there.

One of his paintings in Italy, that of Pope Inocencio X, is also very difficult to reconcile with a cautious, reserved, phlematic personality. Velázquez painted the Pope, an extremely ugly man, just like he looked, complete with his resplendent red and white robes. Apparently the Pope liked it. How would a cautious man paint an ugly Pope?

One should also note that López Jiménez has authentically attributed 123 paintings to Velázquez. In addition, many of his works have been lost and many others are of doubtful authenticity. This seems like a substantial production for a man of phlegmatic personality who was first of all a servant, and secondly a painter, and further indicates how very little we really know about him.

Human personality is complex, and it is always dangerous to try to limit individual characteristics. Probably Velázquez did not talk much because what he had to say was not always favorably received or understood by others. That does not exclude the possibility that occasionally he lost his temper and expressed himself vehemently. He was probably dependable and loyal in view of the fact that he kept his job. To try and pin down his personality more than that seems impossible, unless one does it well aware that he is creating the personality, and that it is the personality of his Velázquez and not that of the Velázquez of history.

That is what Buero does. He chooses to create a rebel who possesses deeper understandings than those with whom he lives, and suffers the loneliness which always accompanies great understanding or sensitivity. Any man who creates anything new, and Velázquez created a new style of painting, is a rebel. Creation of something new always demands rebellion against the old.

Still, in spite of Buero's skill and insight in probing Velázquez' personality, his end product fails to equal that which previous productions lead one to expect. Velázquez is Buero's only "perfect" literary creation, completely void of human frailties. A few human defects would have helped him immensely. No doubt this reflects only an oversight on the author's part, for such characterization is consistent with neither his previous work nor his philosophy. Also, I wonder if Velázquez aloofness was completely justified. The others could not reach up to him, but perhaps he could have reached down to them, if he had felt so inclined.

Although Buero's Velázquez talks plenty and probably more than the true Velázquez, at the same time he cannot communicate with those around him. María Teresa looks up to him because he is older and provides the father image she finds lacking in her own father, but the barrier of age always separates them. He cannot communicate with his wife although he loves her and she loves him. Almost all those with whom he associates are jealous of him, but he is probably the most lonely of all.

However, there is one person with whom he can communicate — Pedro, the old beggar, one of the two ficticious characters. Although Pedro has a more or less minor role in the plot, in the revelation of Velázquez' character his is one of the most important. He reveals Velázquez' loneliness and ideals. Pedro possesses the talent and sensitivity to be a great painter, but because of his awareness of human suffering and sense of responsibility, he sacrifices his life trying to right the wrongs of others.

In remaining loyal to known historical data about these people who lived 300 years ago, Buero has emphasized the universality and timelessness of human nature. Human personalities are no different now than then, and no different than they will be 300 years hence. Society still has people with weak morals, defiant daughters, loyal long-suffering wives, dedicated individuals who sacrifice themselves, and fanatics who want to impose their norms upon others. Customs may change, but human conduct does not seem to improve.

In spite of this universal aspect, one is always tempted to wonder if any particular symbolism is involved. Juan Rodríguez-Castellano interprets the symbolism by saying that the characters represent types of individuals common to Spanish life: Velázquez "represents the nonconformist, the man of superior intelligence who rebels against hypocrisy, narrow-mindedness, and adulation"; Pedro, the people who desire freedom and justice; María Teresa, idealistic rebellious youth; the Marquis, the aristocracy; Martín, the cynic; Juana, the jealous wife who does not understand her husband; and Nieto, "the sinister and envious relative tormented by a puritanic Catholicism." [5] According to his interpretation, the play concerns itself with the relationship of the intelligent nonconformist in Spain with those about him. However, the traits he mentions are universal and not limited to the Spanish culture.

---

[5] *Las Meninas,* ed. Juan Rodríguez-Castellano, New York: Charles Scribner's Sons, 1963, pp. 7-9.

Using stronger words, the play protests a lack of
civil rights, and in so doing incorporates a problem which
transcends the Spanish culture. Although political liberty
can be inherited, it nevertheless remains a privilege which
each generation must earn for itself. It takes only one
generation as morally flabby as the members of Felipe IV's
court to lose privileges which cost their fathers and
grandfathers years to acquire.

The themes of personal liberty and social responsibility
permeate the play. Probably the most forceful expression
of the author's attitude towards the importance of personal
liberty lies in the role of the ex-slave Juan de Pareja,
whom Velázquez had inherited and kept in his house where
he secretly taught him to paint. When it became known
the slave could paint, the King freed him. Everyone re-
marked how clever he had been in deceiving Velázquez
without considering the impossibility of a slave's learning
to paint without his master's knowing it. Towards the
end of the play when Velázquez is trying to learn who
betrayed him to the Inquisition, he questions Pareja and
through Pareja's fearful responses to his questioning, Buero
shows what slavery does to a man's spirit, the jealousy
and resentment which it engenders.

Buero illustrates the hypocrisy resulting when one tries
to restrain another's freedom by the King's double standards in condemning the painting of a nude by a Spaniard
while he himself went from one woman's bed to that of
another and decorated his own bedroom with a nude painted
by the Italian Titian. Italian painters apparently had one
moral standard and Spanish painters another. A parallel
situation has existed since the Civil War with the literary

censorship in Spain. One standard exists for foreign or dead authors and another for the living Spanish.

The liberty just considered has been a political liberty, one which one man may deny another. There is another kind which springs from the heart of man and which no-one can imprison. Velázquez' rebellion exemplifies this second liberty.

Velázquez lived in a court of intrigue and hypocrisy. Everyone was out to feather his own nest and no-one thought of the other fellow's welfare. In order to survive one almost had to adapt. But if one adapts completely, he becomes a slave to his environment. If one does not wish to become a slave to his environment, he must at times rebel. The act of rebelling requires one to demand his liberty, but at the same time he pays a price. Velázquez rebelled from time to time during his lifetime, and he paid with his loneliness. In this play he rebels completely against the King by refusing to destroy his painting of the nude. In that moment he will not yield to his environment and demands his liberty. He risks the price of excommunication and imprisonment. Liberty always carries with it the price of personal responsibility.

During the years prior to this final rebellion before the King Velázquez' attitude vacillated between doubt and faith. When he doubted, he faithfully did his work and insured himself of steady employment in the palace. The moments when he had more faith in himself he defied the others.

One may try to excuse his conduct by saying he did what he did at the King's wishes. The King may have asked him to paint the nude. This argument is weak, however, because Velázquez' painting in general deviated too much from the conservative religious works of the past. It seems more likely that through his painting he was probing the meaning of truth, trying to exceed the conventions of his time and discover something more, like Buero.

Buero raises the question of the meaning of truth no less than eight times during the play, thus making it one of the most important of those presented.

VELÁZQUEZ:	*(to María Teresa)* You are 18 years old. I'm 56. If people knew I was telling you the truth, nobody would understand... Truth is a terrible burden: the price is loneliness. And in the Court nobody, do you hear, nobody, asks to hear the truth.
MARÍA TERESA:	I want to hear the truth.
VELÁZQUEZ:	Perhaps you're not making the best choice. Your kind will rarely permit you to find it, although you may have your eyes open. They'll close them again for you. (p. 68)
PEDRO:	*(to Velázquez)* One day you said: things change... Perhaps their truth may be in their appearance which also changes.
VELÁZQUEZ:	You remember that?
PEDRO:	I think you said: if we succeed in looking at them in a different way than the ancients, we could even paint the sensation of space. (p. 78)
PEDRO:	I'm old, Don Diego. I'll live only a little while longer and I wonder what certainty the world has given me... Now I only know I'm just a bit of sick flesh, full of fear and waiting to die. A tired man in search of a little wisdom that will let him rest from this strange madness before dying. (p. 80)

VELÁZQUEZ: I don't know how to say it. I believe that
               truth... is in those simple moments more than
               in etiquette... Then all can be loved... the
               dog, the dwarfs, the little girl... (p. 95)

PEDRO: *(speaking of the sketch of* Las Meninas)
               They're living ghosts of persons whose truth
               is death. (p. 101)

VELÁZQUEZ: Pedro, is the world truly horrible?...
PEDRO: Take these words of mine with you for they
               may be the last that you'll hear from me.
               Since you're going to confront lies and false-
               hoods, lie for the sake of your work, if
               need be, for that is true. (p. 131)

VELÁZQUEZ: *(to the King)* One thing more, sir. I
               understand what you are asking of me. Loyal
               words that cost nothing... Who knows what
               we're thinking? If I pronounce them I may
               paint what I should paint, and your Majesty
               will listen to the lie you want to hear to
               keep you content.
KING: What are you saying?
VELÁZQUEZ: It's a choice, sir. On one hand the lie one
               more time. A tempting lie: it can only be to
               my advantage. On the other hand, the truth.
               A dangerous truth that won't remedy anything.
               If Pedro Briones were alive, he'd repeat what
               he told me before I came here: lie if need
               be. You should paint. But he has died. *(His
               voice breaks.)* He has died. What is your
               cunning worth compared to his death? What
               can I give in order to be worthy of him,
               if he has given his life? I can no longer lie,
               even though I should. His death prevents it. I
               offer you my futile truth... *(Vibrant)* The
               truth, sir, of my profound, my irremediable
               rebellion. (p. 163)

KING: Watch your words!

VELÁZQUEZ: Not now, sir. Hunger increases; suffering
                   increases; the air is poisoned and does not
                   even tolerate the truth which must hide itself
                   like my Venus, because it is naked. Rather
                   I should speak it. We are living on lies or
                   silence. I've lived silently, but I refuse to
                   lie. (p. 164)

These quotations contain three fundamental ideas about
truth which appear time and again in Buero's work. First
is his insistence upon truth from the time of his very
first play, *Ardiente*. But, as he has Velázquez say to
María Teresa, nobody wants to hear the truth, only lies,
and after a while people become so accustomed to living
their lies they cannot recognize the truth when they do
see or hear it. And this is the second idea fundamental
in Buero's writing. Man becomes blind to the truth and
his situation. The third concept is that man's only truth
is death.

The conflict between Velázquez and the King and
Pedro's death further develop the points just mentioned.
For example, weak old Pedro is nearly blind because of
his age, but still he seems at times to perceive things
through some sort of a sixth sense similar to that found
in such works as *Hoy es fiesta* and *La señal que se espera*.
Velázquez takes him to look at his sketch of *Las Meninas*
although he is aware of Pedro's lack of sight and knows
that probably he can not see it. In one of the most
interesting scenes of the play, however, he does see it.

PEDRO: Yes, I think I understand. A serene picture, but
                   containing all the sadness of Spain. Anyone who
                   sees these creatures will understand how irredeem-

ably condemned they are to suffer. They're living ghosts whose truth is death. Whoever sees them in the future will notice it with terror. Yes, with terror, until there comes a moment, as is happening with me now, until he will not know if perhaps he is not the ghost before the gazes of these figures... And he will want to save himself from them, embark upon the immovable ship of this room, since they're looking at him, since he's then in the picture and they're looking at him... And perhaps, while he seeks his own face in the mirror at the back, he will save himself for a moment from dying. *(He presses his eyes with his fingers.)* Forgive me... I should talk to you of colors, like a painter, but now I can't. I scarcely see. I'm probably saying very stupid things about your picture. I've arrived late to enjoy it.

VELÁZQUEZ: *(Who has listened to him, greatly moved.)* No, Pedro. This canvas was waiting for you. Your eyes fuse the crudeness of the sketch and already see the large picture... just as I'll try to paint it. A picture of miserable men saved by light... I've come to suspect that the very form of God, if he has one, would be light. It cures me of all the insanities of this world. Suddenly, I see, and peace envelopes me.

PEDRO: You see?

VELÁZQUEZ: Anything at all: a corner, the facial coloring of a profile... and a terrible emotion possesses me, and then a complete calm. Then, that passes... and I don't know how I could enjoy such beatuty in midst of such suffering. (pp. 101-102)

This one scene expresses, intuitively, the whole tragic concept of the human situation.

The actual climax of the play occurs later when Velázquez has been accused of painting an immoral picture

and has learned of Pedro's death. He then rebels against
the King. The King wants words of flattery which he
refuses to give. In the end Velázquez wins, and the King
forgives him. In these moments the tragic tension reaches
its highest peak; the conflict between liberty and social
necessity, doubt and faith, becomes so strong that Velázquez must make a choice. Pedro's death provides him
with the truth he had been seeking.

If death, as Pedro has said, is the only truth, what
does that mean? Should one spend his lifetime preparing
for death? If so, how? What is the secret of death? In
almost every great work I have read I have felt the secret
of death was love, and I feel this is true of Buero's work
also. In this particular case, when Velázquez learned that
Pedro had died, he realized how much he had loved him.
This love was so great that he felt not only the injustices
which Pedro had received, but also those of all like him.
He had to rebel because he could no longer tolerate the
hypocrisy which created these injustices. He became aware
of his love for his fellow man, a love to which previously
he had been blind, and to which he still remained blind
as far as its meaning was concerned. Expressed in a
different way, through death he became aware of the value
of life. This awareness may be a definition of love.

At the same time, this moment of tragic climax
demanded an act of faith. It demanded a faith in something
more than the superficiality of the court — a faith in his
own ability to resist and overcome evil, in an unknown
truth which transcends human existence on earth. A faith
which he found in death.

After such a lengthy consideration of the play, a summary of the characteristics which make it Buero's most representative play might be in order.

Although his dramatic technique varies from play to play, from the almost complete omission of action to the inclusion of violence, this play demonstrates Buero's skill in creating dramatic situations as well as any. The aesthetic qualities of the costuming and of the tableau at the end equal those of any prior work.

The historical accuracy illustrates Buero's attention to details as well as the timelessness and universality of his characters. Everything from beggars to Negro slaves to strong dynamic personalities like Velázquez and Princess María Teresa walk across the stage. Typically, the most philosophical lines and the greatest psychic strength spring forth from the physically and socially weakest character — old, nearly blind Pedro. Although the characters come from history, in reality they are contemporary and universal individuals with memorable personalities rather than types.

Buero's sympathetic recognition of man's physical limitations is portrayed by Pedro and the dwarfs. Pedro also symbolizes through the theme of blindness man's inability to see and understand his predicament.

The tragic attitude is reflected in the lives of the characters and climaxed in Pedro's death. Pedro and Velázquez present the theme of personal responsibility, a theme frequently arriving as it does here to the point of rebellion in Buero's work. Inclusion of the ex-slave Juan Pareja emphasizes the theme of liberty. Rejection of the King's promiscuous behavior is consistent with Buero's high moral tone. Hypocrisy is attacked when Velázquez' friends betray him.

The play is popular in the sense that it is written for the man in the street and considers his problems; intellectual in that it remains true to accepted academic knowledge; and a play of ideas in that it presents different facets of the problems of evil, social responsibility, morality, liberty, and truth, all problems of our time, and leaves them for the reader or spectator to resolve.

EL CONCIERTO DE SAN OVIDIO

F R O M the traditional Aristotelian point of view *El concierto de San Ovidio* would be Buero's most powerful tragedy. From Buero's point of view it is the play which most persistently seeks a reason for human suffering and responds with the strongest expression of faith. Juan Emilio Aragonés in commenting the play in *La Estafeta Literaria* acclaimed it as "the first great tragedy of the Spanish theater of all time." [1]

The play is based on a little known incident in French history which took place in 1771 in Paris. In the play Luis María Valindin takes six beggars from a home for the blind and presents them as a stage show in the carnival of San Ovidio. He creates the sensation of the carnival by dressing them in ridiculous costumes and mocking their handicap. Contenting themselves with full bellies, five of the six adjust to the derision of the spectators. The sixth, David, finds Valindin's cruelty too much to bear and kills him. He is apprehended and hung for his crime. The

---

[1] Federico Carlos Sáinz de Robles, ed., *Teatro Español 1962-1963*, Madrid: Aguilar, 1964, p. 75.

stupid, ridiculous spectacle transcends the suffering of the participants, however, and inspires Valentin Haüy to establish a school for the blind. His student Luis Braille later continues his work.

AN ARISTOTELIAN TRAGEDY

From an Aristotelian viewpoint, the play is an imitation of a serious, complete action, as Aristotle says tragedy should be. It can be considered independently of the characters, for the events in themselves continue in a logical manner increasing in dramatic tension and climaxing in the murder of Valindin. The imitation of an action appears completely logical, understandable, and plausible. The language used effects "through pity and terror the correction and refinement of such passions." [2] Regardless of how one interprets what Aristotle may have meant by this catharsis, it occurs. The spectator may begin with pity and fear for the blind, but by the end of the play this pity and fear have been broadened to encompass not only the blind but also those who see. At the same time the play removes pity and fear, for the spectator sees that the suffering of the blind has a meaning and purpose in as much as it serves as inspiration for Haüy. Purification, or catharsis, also occurs in the actors. David loses his fear as the play evolves to assume personal responsibility and make atonement in the end by killing Valendin. A curious mixture of love and hate leads him to do this. The play

---

[2] Benjamin Jowett and Thomas Twining, trans., *Aristotle's Politics and Poetics*, New York: The Viking Press, 1959, p. 230.

also fulfills Buero's concept of catharsis, the transformation of pity into reflective compassion before human suffering, and fear into sacred terror before the powers of the universe.

Although the psychologies and personalities of the characters are developed, as one expects in a play of the twentieth century, at the same time David contains much of the Aristotelian hubristic hero. In fact, pride brings about his downfall, for he cannot content himself to be a blind animal. He insists that one day he will read, write, play music, and love like those who see. This pride, springing in grand part from his intellect, compels him to defy Valindin. He could not do otherwise.

Although pride brings about his destruction, it also brings about his spiritual salvation. The conflict between Valindin and David becomes so great that Valindin intends to have David imprisoned. David learns this. No longer can he continue dreaming and hoping. He must act. Circumstances force him to choose between resisting or becoming one of the living dead in jail. Life offers him no easy out on a psychiatrist's couch.

Paradoxically, David's hamartia or blind spot lies in that he can see in spite of his blindness. He anticipates events. With the exception of Haüy, only David believes the blind will learn to do all the things others do. In a splendid scene at the end of the first act he tells Adriana, Valindin's mistress, that she will be rewarded with a new dress or a jewel for helping arrange the ridiculous spectacle of blind beggars, and that she will use her feminine charms to deceive them. When he leaves, Valindin enters, urges her to play with the emotions of the blind, particularly those of Donato, the young teen-age boy, and they practically repeat the previous conversation between David and Adriana. She realizes the irony of the situation, but only laughs.

Another example of David's foresight occurs in the second act. Adriana and the blind beggars await him before going to the booth at the fair. He has gone to visit a student friend to ask him the symbolic meanings of certain birds. When they arrive at the festival, we learn that David's intuition had told him Valindin would make fools of them by using a peacock to decorate the bandstand. That is exactly what happens. The peacock represents the mythological symbol of stupidity and folly. It was painted at the side of the imbecile King Midas, who was born with the ears of a donkey.

David's keen perception, his ability to learn his way around the rooms quickly, his complete control of his use of the cane, and finally his murder of Valindin complete this portrayal of a blind man who sees.

Still, with a different temperament David could have perhaps used this wit and cunning for purely selfish motives and perhaps survived. He could have heartily joined in the endeavor and devoted his energies to conniving schemes for stealing Valindin blind. However, his sensibility prevents this. Coupled with keen perception, this sensibility and his passions drive him to his doom. David loves.

He loves Adriana, Valindin's mistress, and the fatherless teen-ager Donato. Although single and childless, he possesses the sentiments of a family man. Adriana in order to help Valindin control the beggars makes a play for Donato and finally seduces him. Donato discovers the deception and the love between Adriana and David. Jealously he betrays David to the police. Another paradox of the human situation. Moral virtue, or love, terminates in murder and betrayal.

Nevertheless, the plays ends on a note of reconciliation. David is hung; Donato spends the rest of his life wandering the street haunted by his memories; but others, because of their misfortunes, enjoy a better life created through the endeavors of Haüy. Buero does not attempt to explain the events theologically or philosophically, or to tell us who is to blame for David and Valindin's deaths. He offers only a reconciliation of opposing forces, thus expressing faith that life with all its suffering must have some meaning. He himself would be quick to add that he has not indicated where this faith lies — in God or in man.

A SOCIAL TRAGEDY

As a social tragedy *Concierto* shows man's inability to overcome on any but the individual level a morally corrupt society. The most obvious source of moral corruption in the play lies in Valindin, whom Buero has said he intented to represent an incipient exploitative capitalism operating under the guise of philanthropy.

The exposure of this ficticious philanthropy begins with an attack on organized religion. Buero changes history to place the home for blind beggars under religious rather than civil management. The Sister who manages the home appears pious, but the beggars know she eats better than they do. Fully aware of Valindin's reputation, in return for her financial gain she permits the unseeing blind to leave her protection and serve him. With spiritual rather than material motivation she would have defended them from him. Like Doña Pepita in *Ardiente,* she can see but refuses to open her eyes. Only after receiving Valindin's final payment does she wash her hands of him.

In return for the financial benefits received from Valindin, the beggars pray for his soul, for as the Prioress says, all commercial enterprize lies beneath the dignity of the home. Beggars were made only to pray. Here again one notes Buero's irony.

Throughout the play Valindin repeatedly insists he is a philanthropist operating under the protection of the nobility. The social implications seem quite clear. Like the Prioress, he also quickly points out how much he does for others, but those who work for him, those he supposedly helps most, hate and fear him. Still, they depend upon him for their livelihood. None can escape.

As a philanthropist and like the church Valindin is a conservative. When he first meets the Prioress he tells her how the world is opening up new roads of knowledge and wealth, but he like her will never recognize the writings of Rousseau or Voltaire. Instead he relies upon the holy truths of his elders and the protection of the nobility. Voltaire directed the battle against intolerance and fanaticism in France while Rousseau was a sentimental deist with sentimentality the essence and deism the accident of his creed. Thus in these very few lines Buero defines the attitude and character of his philanthopist.

As the play progresses more seemingly innocent sentences loaded with social implications appear, as for example later on in the first act when Valindin tells Adriana he is a good — hearted philanthropist, but "philanthropy is also the fountain of wealth." (p. 25) In the home the beggars had been slowly dying of hunger, but now Valindin will be their protector. Spiritual death as beneficiaries of a charity replaces physical death for hungry beggars. Everything revolves about financial enterprise.

The sight of the blind beggars on the bandstand with the peacock background accentuates the tragic situation of the unfortunate. As previously mentioned, the peacock symbolizes stupidity. Gilberto, a mentally retarded meningitis victim, portrays the idiot King Midas. The horrible dissonance ridicules the musical efforts of the group, and the spectators are unaware that Valindin has forbidden even the attempt of a professional performance. As one of the spectators points out, the spectacle represents vanity. But the vanity of whom? Of the uneducated trying the impossible, or the vanity of one who considers himself superior to others?

In considering the problems of the unfortunate, Buero offers several solutions. The crudest lies in killing them as the Germans did in World War II, as Donato's father wanted to do to his son, and as Valindin says they do in Madagascar (p. 64).

Another solution lies in resignation. As Buero points out through the words of Donato, some consider blindness, and this implies the accompanying poverty, as the will of God. David does not think so (p. 39). And here again one finds a basic question occuring throughout all Buero's work. How much can man do to improve his situation, and how much must he accept with resignation?

Another approach to the problem suggests poverty may be the root of the evil. David heard of the blind lady Melania de Salignac (p. 19) who could read and write, but the blind men know she must me very rich, for only the rich would have such an opportunity. The blind beggars

agree to Valindin's demands because doing so provides
them with food. Adriana and the other employees remain
with him because they are financially dependent upon him.
Physical poverty imposes   certain limitations upon what
these people can do, and before great strides can be made
in correcting moral problems, such abject poverty may
have to be eliminated. Buero does not care to recognize
that anything can limit man in his efforts to improve
himself spiritually, but he does admit that extreme poverty
might do so. He also doubts that these people would have
been greatly different morally even though their financial
situation had been otherwise.

Valindin thinks he is removing poverty when he
provides work for the beggars. He introduces them to the
public pointing out what philanthropy can do for mankind
— how it can channel human energy into constructive
activities and provide gainful employment which removes
beggars from the streets. In this case the employment
consists of providing comic entertainment which, he says,
is not a bad thing. Men have honored jesters and clowns
since the beginning of time. Laughter helps one forget the
cares of the world. "All of us laugh at everyone; the world
is a great carnival." (p. 63) But who laughs at whom?
As Haüy points out when he leaves the show, perhaps
the real clowns are the audience, the ones who laugh
loudest. And what is the effect of this laughter? Does it
perhaps slowly change into revulsion before the tragic
spectacle on the stage? Economic solutions seem to fall
flat on their face as a complete, permanent solution to
resolving the problems of the unfortunate.

And so the question returns to that of individual
responsibility. In order to accept this responsibility, one

must possess the necessary freedom to do so. Rather than talk about personal liberty directly, though, Buero implies the theme through the conflict between David and Valindin, who denies David the right to try to teach the others to play the violin. He even takes away David's violin so he cannot use it to console himself. While the others resign themselves to being little more than trained animals, David can not. Here one sees the parallel to the role of the artist in contemporary society with the various types of controls and censorhips which exist throughout the world. Buero adds, however, that he is not talking only about the artist or writer. Any oppressive force can take away the tools by which any worker gains his livelihood leaving the individual as helpless in deciding his destiny as the heroes of the Greek tragedies were against the powerful forces which controlled their fate.

A PERSONAL TRAGEDY

The analysis up to now has considered mainly the external social factors which contributed to the tragedy. Considering the work from a psychological point of view, fear appears as the underlying force. When the blind learn the true nature of their musical production, they want to leave, but Valindin's threat of prison forces them to stay. The carpenter endures Valindin's cruelties in order to support his small boy who is afraid of the dark. Afraid of an unknown future, Adriana stays with Valindin. Because of fear Valindin laughs and David dreams. Near the end of the play David tells Valindin:

DAVID: You've taught me a lesson and I'd like to express
               my appreciation to you. When the Prioress told us
               about you, I said to myself: "At last! I'll help that
               man and I'll venerate him all my life." Later... I
               understood that it had to do with making laughter.
               But after all, all of us are clowns. Thanks for
               having converted me into a clown. It has been an
               unforgettable experience.

VALINDIN: You amuse me, goofball.

DAVID: I'm glad! To amuse is the best thing. "The little
               sheep bleat: baa, baa, baa..."

VALINDIN: Crazy, man, crazy.

DAVID: It's the only way to free one's self from fear. Well,
               there's another way, but it's only for a few. Most
               people have to jump about like little animals at a
               carnival in order to quiet their fear. Or make
               themselves dream...

VALINDIN: Oh, and that secret?

DAVID: I'll tell you pretty soon. As I was saying, I used
               to dream in order to forget my fear. I dreamed with
               music, and that I loved a woman I didn't even
               know. And I also dreamed nobody would hurt me
               and I wouldn't hurt anybody else... What a dreamer!
               Right? To dare dream such things in a world where
               they can starve us to death or change us into circus
               clowns, or beat us... or put us in jail for life with
               a secret letter. It was like beating a tired horse.
               (pp. 100-101)

As the play progresses David learns that while
dreaming and laughing provide escape from fear, a better
alternative is to confront it. When he did this, he found
the courage to kill Valindin. Reflection can direct human
efforts into constructive channels, such as Haüy's teaching
the blind. By killing Valindin and ridding the world of
one evil, David responded to his fear in the only apparent
positive way, and in so doing overcame it.

Action, the alternative to dreaming and laughter, expresses the faith inherent in the work. As the author says, even the most insignificant of men can work miracles if he but believe. (p. 142) To further emphasize the faith inherent in the work, he has based it on an historical incident. History proves man can indeed work miracles.

This alternative to running from fear raises the question of guilt. Who was to blame for all the human suffering revealed in this play? If poverty and ignorance had been removed, would something inherent within Valindin and David still have led them to this conflict? If they had not been dependent upon each other, would they have adopted an attitude of live and let live? The play seems to express Buero's opinion at the end when Haüy asks himself who was responsible for the two deaths.

Sure, I'm opening up a new life for the blind children I teach; but if they hung one of those blind men, who assumes the responsibility for his death? Who redeems it? I'm old. When I don't see anybody, like now, I like to imagine at times if perhaps... music, may be the only answer possible for some questions. (p. 112)

L I K E *Madrugada, Aventura en lo gris* breaks away
from traditional concepts of tragedy. The "strong" characters are the "weak" ones, and while probably the point
of greatest dramatic tension occurs at the end of the play,
tension does not steadily progress to this point. Rather,
events seem to converge at the end from two different
directions, the first act and the dream interlude.

Like the social dramas, the play comments contemporary problems and shows man because of egoism and
indifference caught up in an inescapable web of destructive
events.

Also, while in one sense Buero follows his usual careful,
well-planned construction, at the same time this play is
more mythical and abstract than the others.

The action takes place in a lodging for refugees in
Surelia, an imaginary European country. The first act
begins during the evening as the refugees enter to spend
the night. They include a laborer, a rich tourist, a soldier, the dictator of Surelia and his mistress traveling incog-
nito, a professor from the University, and two young people with a baby. A dream scene follows the first act and

the second act takes place the next morning as the refugees prepare to leave the shelter. During the night while the others dream, the dictator kills Isabel, the girl with the baby. The young man accompanying her then kills the dictator. While the others escape to the border, the dictator's mistress and the professor save the baby by staying to give it to the approaching enemy soldiers. Because of the distance to the border and the lack of food, escape with the infant would have been impossible. Sparing the child, the enemy soldiers shoot the dictator's mistress and the professor. The only hope for the future lies not in lofty ideals or among the high born, but with this half-starved, helpless offspring of a teen-ager and an enemy soldier. As indicated by this summary of the plot, the main theme of the play has to do with the facility with which a modern nation can fall victim to a dictator.

Since this is Buero's only play which considers war directly, one may feel tempted to let his imagination run away with itself in developing the symbolism within the work. However, care should be used in relating it to the Spanish Civil War. While the censorship leads one to wonder what lies hidden between the lines, with Buero the answer is usually not too much. If he has something to say, he will say it clearly, as in expressing his ideas about democracy in *Soñador*. In commenting on this play he has said that his only intention was to present a universal problem, and he doubted if he was thinking of Franco even subconsciously. All the events are ficticious and no definite relationship exists with any specific political or social situation. And furthermore, while this may be the only play which considers war in a contemporary setting, the theme has certainly been treated indirectly before, as in *Tejedora,* the conflict between Ignacio and the school in *Ardiente,* and in *Soñador.*

Rather than become too involved with the symbolism and the Spanish Civil War, one would do better to consider the basic moral intention of the work as brought out through the characterization. The play contains only two seemingly innocent people—Isabel and the baby. Buero, however, would say that even these are not innocent. He envisions guilt in a baby as existing in physical and psychical limitations which will cause him to commit antisocial acts as he matures.

Georgiana, the tourist, represents a negative factor within the country—one who comes to take advantage of the excellent tourist facilities at exceedingly low prices and indifferent to the wants and needs of the people there. She has no qualms about exploiting others, and in the play is eager to take the farmer's food and gratify her sexual desires with the mentally unbalanced Carlos.

The farmer is little more than an animal. Only his instinct for survival enables him to continue on and to eat his bread while the others watch. Cruelty and suffering have numbed his senses until he no longer feels anything.

Carlos represents a more complex reaction to human suffering. When he joined the army he accepted Goldmann's words as "right" because they sounded good and added excitement to his life. As Silvano tells him,

You have fought because you could not live without a leader, and your leader ordered you to fight. Because you do not know how to live without beautiful words, and Goldmann provided you with that rhetoric in big doses. (p. 31)

However, the war changes that. He reacts emotionally to the violence. Isabel's death brings him to seek revenge during a moment of passion. In addition, the murder brought about the release of suppressed pent-up sexual frustrations. His act while moral was also biological.

Ana, Goldman's mistress, committed another bio-moral act of personal responsibility. For years she lived with Goldmann enduring his crudeness and infidelities, although essentially she herself was not cruel. She secretly gave bread, for example, to the others, after he had forbidden it. At the end of the play she rebels against his cruelties and accepts her own personal responsibilities by staying with Silvano and trying to save the baby, knowing full well the consequences may be rape or death. She didn't have to stay. She could have left and accepted the attentions due a faithful secretary. Or she could have seen his murderer brought to justice. Instead, she chooses to make restitution.

Buero himself does not see her motive as being quite that simple. The basis of her action for him is frustrated motherhood. He envisions an Ana who for years avoided Goldmann, refusing to give him the son he wanted. He seems to forget that Goldmann had refused to make their relationship legal, but assumes that in spite of her apparent goodness she feels guilty because of this failure to produce a son. Her reaction to this feeling of guilt is the attempt to save Isabel's baby. For Buero the suppressed biological craving exceeds the moral qualities of her act.

While Ana and Carlos react more or less out of instint and passion in accepting their responsibilities, Silvano assumes his through a more reflective, thoughtful approach. He too had compromised with his environment, but instead of trying to fool himself into thinking it was morally acceptable, he "dreamed." True, because of his dreams he was able to expose Goldmann, but nevertheless Goldmann had acquired his power because of the lethargy and indifference of those like Silvano. And Isabel was murdered while everybody dreamed. Like Ana, Silvano feels within himself a frustrated desire for parenthood, but because of the more reflective nature of his character, he reacts to this urge with his head instead of his heart.

The dream scene from an aesthetic point of view is very impressive and reflects the author's artistic training. During the first and second acts the walls of the lodging are grey and the characters dress in greys and neutral tones. The only colorful object is a red, white, and blue poster of Goldmann, the dictator. In the dream scene the walls have become an indefinite panorama of a marine scene with vague forms of corals and sea animals. Silvano has changed his grey suit for black rags; Ana's nondescript suit has been replaced by a nurse's uniform; Carlos wears the same clothes as before but they are a bright red; Georgiana wears a night-gown; the farmer has an expensive suit complete with a gold chain and medallion on the jacket; medals cover the chest of the sergeant's uniform; and Isabel, barefooted, wears a white shirt. This colorful contrast to the drabness of the other two scenes suggests that while life may be colorless, the dreams may be as bright as can be. The title, as the author has indicated, carries through this same idea. One can find adventure in the greyness and monotony of life. The question is, where does one find the adventure? Which is the reality, the greyness of life, or the gaudiness of the dreams? Or perhaps they are two parts of the same thing.

The author does not clarify just exactly where life's adventure lies, but he has this to say about dreams.

SILVANO: To learn to dream would be to learn to live. All of us dream with our unconfessable appetites and during the night we let loose the wild beast that possesses us. But if we would learn... Do we dream badly because we behave badly during the day, or do we proceed badly in life because we do not know how to dream well? It isn't easy to answer, is it?... Perhaps both are true. But then, one also needs to learn to dream... Only... we don't learn. For that reason sometimes I think something... very strange. If the people who associate with one another should begin to dream regularly the same dream?... It isn't possible. It would suffice that our minds should become something more flexible in order to send or capture thoughts.

ALEJANDRO: Telepathy?

SILVANO: Something like that. Then dreams would be like a prolongation of life, but more naked, more impressionistic. We would dream the same and the clash of our egoisms would make them impossible. We would see ourselves as we are inside and perhaps when we awoke we could not continue pretending. We would have to force ourselves to improve... Because we touch our true depth in dreaming. (pp. 44-45)

            ... To act through commissions, governments, and congresses will not help much if our united dreams do not lead us. (p. 97)

The action itself does not seem to bear out these words too strongly, and this may be a defect of the play. All except Goldmann dream together. While they dream he kills Isabel. The dream itself presents no fixed conclusions, but rather emits from the vague, illusory qualities of the human subconsciousness. The mythical abstractness leaves the interpretation extremely open.

The easiest explanation of the dream is that the body continues its normal functions during sleep with the mind never really resting. The refugees show the same pettiness dreaming as when awake. At the same time, in their dreams they lose some of the reserve evident during their waking hours. Although still greedy, they exhibit more fear and guilt. The dream expresses Carlos' feelings of guilt and sexual frustration, Ana's compassion, the sergeant's craving for power, Isabel's fear, and so on.

The dream also reveals the common human bonds which bind them together, bonds of which they are not aware and the existence of which they would not believe even if they were told of them. These human bonds would always exist in conflict with the selfishness exhibited in the dream as they divided the bread. The paradox of life—we are all in it together, but instead of cooperating with each other, we exhaust our energies frustrating one another.

The dream scene also suggests that dreams precede action, as stated in the passage quoted. In the dream Carlos is as confused and feels as guilty as he does the following morning when he learns that Isabel is dead. The sergeant directs the activities of the others as he would the next day as they prepare to leave the shelter. Georgiana tries to seduce Carlos, and the next day she tells him she will care for him. Ana wants to help and later she helps Silvano save the baby.

Still another idea suggested by the dream is that dreams distort reality. Events do not seem as well organized and logical in the dream as in the two main acts. Still, the dream is a part of reality and as much a part of the living experience of these individuals as their waking hours and the beating of their hearts. Perhaps dreams may be the logical, well-organized part of life, and the waking hours the distorted.

Of all the refugees, only Silvano remembers his dream. Ana vaguely recalls something but she cannot remember exactly what. Why is Silvano the only one to remember? Does he possess a sensitivity others do not possess, or does he dream because he is so completely dissatisfied with the human situation that in dreaming he finds the only means to escape?

While in one sense this dream leaves the reader somewhat unsatisfied because of its lack of explicitness, still it represents an important aspect of Buero's work. First, he recognizes that everything cannot be explained in articulate terms. Some things have to be sensed and accepted in all their vagueness and incomprehensibility. Also, the scene represents one of the author's attempts to stretch the limits of artistic expression and express the inexpressible. Only time can judge Buero's success with this method of probing the depths of the human soul.

CONCLUSION

A N artist has only three basic themes with which he can work, society, the individual, and the metaphysical. Buero uses all of these.

In developing the social theme he has written dramas which portray realistically current life and customs within Spain. These plays analyze social problems as much as the censorship and artistic expression permit. In an attempt to further clarify and understand these problems, in his later work he has turned to their historical backgrounds, thus explaining current situations in terms of historical antecedents.

In considering the individual, he shows not only the relationship with society, but also more personal ones within the family. This sociological representation is further clarified by a psychological consideration of the different facets of human personality.

His approach to the universe is essentially tragic, although personal responsibility far outweighs the inherent fatalism. Moral improvement seems to be the principal means for acquiring a more spiritually satisfying life. A strong sense of guilt, the strongest indication of the Christian influence in his work, appears from time to time.

In exploring these three basic themes, Buero directs his work toward the man in the street. He expresses himself clearly and directly in correct conversational Spanish. At the same time, because of the careful construction and complexities of thought, his plays contain many subtleties. The reflective quality contrasts with situations at times highly dramatic. Recognizing the limitations of the word, he employs aesthetic means to transmit the greater truths. The experimental aspect of his work lies not so much in trying to say in a new way what others have already said, but rather in trying to express what has never been said before, to stretch the limits of artistic expression to express the inexpressible.

In short, Buero is an artist who wants to be master of his art.

BIBLIOGRAPHY

Dramatic Works by Antonio Buero Vallejo

Except for *Las Meninas,* editions published by Escelicer, S. A. (Madrid) were used for this study. The number of the edition used is indicated in parenthesis. For *Las Meninas* the edition by Charles Scribner's Sons (New York) was used. It has also been published by Escelicer. At times slight variations are found between different editions, but these have not been considered in this study. The date listed after each work is that of its premier in Madrid.

Historia de una escalera. October 14, 1949 (4th edition). Lope de Vega Prize in 1949. Other editions: José Janés, ed., Barcelona: Colección manantial que no cesa, 1950; *Teatro Español 1949-1950,* Madrid: Aguilar, S. A., 1951; José Sánchez, ed., New York: Charles Scribner's Sons, 1955; in an anthology by Losada, Buenos Aires, 1962; Introduction, notes and vocabulary by H. Lester and J. A. Zalalbeascoa, London: University of London Press, 1963; in an anthology by Escelicer, Madrid, 1966.

Las palabras en la arena. December 19, 1949 (4th edition). First Prize of "Amigos de los Quintero," 1949.

En la ardiente oscuridad. December 1, 1950 (4th edition). Other editions: *Teatro Español 1950-1951,* Madrid: Aguilar, S. A., 1952; Samuel A. Wofsy, ed., New York: Charles Scribner's Sons, 1954; in an anthology by Losada, Buenos Aires, 1959.

La tejedora de sueños. January 11, 1952 (1st edition). Also published in an anthology by Losada, Buenos Aires, 1962.

Casi un cuento de hadas. January 9, 1952 (1st edition).

La señal que se espera. May 21, 1952 (2nd edition).

Madrugada. December 9, 1953 (2nd edition). Other editions: *Teatro Español 1953-1954,* Madrid: Aguilar, S. A., 1955; in an anthology by Losada, Buenos Aires, 1959.

Irene, o el tesoro. December 14, 1954 (1st edition). Also published in an anthology by Losada, Buenos Aires, 1962.

Hoy es fiesta. September 20, 1956 (2nd edition). María Rolland Prize, 1956; National Theatre Prize, 1957; March Prize,

1959. Other editions: J. E. Lyon, ed., vocabulary by K. S. B. Croft, London: George G. Harrap and Co., Ltd., 1964; in an anthology by Losada, Buenos Aires, 1959.

Las cartas boca abajo. November 5, 1957 (2nd edition). National Theater Prize, 1958. Other editions: *Teatro Español 1957-1958*, Madrid: Aguilar, S. A., 1959; in an anthology by Losada, Buenos Aires, 1959; in an anthology by Escelicer, Madrid, 1966; Félix G. Ilárraz, ed., New York: Prentice-Hall, 1967.

Un soñador para un pueblo. December 18, 1958 (1st edition). María Rolland Prize, 1958; National Theater Prize, 1959; Critics' Prize of Barcelona, 1960. Other editions: in an anthology by Losada, Buenos Aires, 1959; *Teatro Español 1958-1959*, Madrid: Aguilar, S. A., 1960; in an anthology by Escelicer, Madrid, 1966; M. Manzanares de Cirre, ed., New York: Charles Scribner's Sons, 1967.

Las Meninas. December 9, 1960 (1st edition). María Rolland Prize, 1960. Other editions: Juan Rodríguez-Castellano, ed., New York: Charles Scribner's Sons, 1963; in an anthology by Escelicer, Madrid, 1966.

Hamlet, Príncipe de Dinamarca. December 14, 1961 (1st edition).

El concierto de San Ovidio. November 16, 1962 (1st edition). Larra Prize, 1961-62. Other editions: Prologue by Jean Paul Borel, Aymá, 1963; *Teatro Español 1962-1963*, Madrid: Aguilar, S. A., 1964; P. N. Trakas, ed., New York: Charles Scribner's Sons, 1965; in an anthology by Escelicer, Madrid, 1966.

Aventura en lo gris. October 1, 1963 (1st edition).

El terror inmóvil. This play has never been presented. The second act was published in 1954 in *Número 100*, an anthology published by Escelicer, Madrid.

Translations

Although various sources indicate that Buero's plays have been translated into English, French, Italian, German, Slavic, and Ukrainian, the following are the only ones I have found listed in the bibliographical sources consulted.

ANTONIO BUERO VALLEJO   185

ARDREY, ROBERT. "La Tour d'ivoire." Adap. de Jean Mercure,
  prés. par Paul-Louis Mignon. Théâtre des Bouffes-Parisiens,
  2 oct. 1958.

BOOTY, JILL, trans. "The Story of a Staircase."

CAMP, JEAN. "Ecrit su le sable." L'Avant Scène, Fémina-théâtre,
  183.

OLIVER, WM. I., trans. "The Weaver of Dreams" published in
  The Genius of the Spanish Theater. Robert O'Brien, ed.
  New York: Mentor, 1964.

WOFSEY, SAMUEL F. and THEODORE HATLEN, trans. "In the
  Burning Darkness."

LITERARY CRITICISM

ABELLÁN, JOSÉ LUIS. "El tema de misterio en Buero Vallejo:
  Un teatro de la realidad trascendente." Insula. xvi, clxxiv, 15.

ALFONSO, CARMEN. "Buero Vallejo: 'Las Meninas.'" *Mujeres
  en la Isla*. lxxxiv (Palma de Gran Canaria, 1961), 9.

ÁLVAREZ, C. L. "Un Velázquez de ocasión." *Índice*. xii, cxlv, 27.

ALVAR, FRANCISCO. *El espectador y la crítica*. Valladolid: Ta-
  lleres Gráficos Ceres, 1960.

"Antonio Buero Vallejo Answers Seven Questions." *Theater
  Annual*. xix (1962), 1-6.

ARCE, C. DE. "Buero Vallejo." *Virtud y Letras*. xv, lx (Bogotá,
  1956), 419-30.

ATLEE, ALFRED FRANCIS. "The Social-Political Ethic in the
  Plays of Antonio Buero Vallejo Produced and Published from
  October, 1949 to October, 1963," Ph.D. thesis, University
  of Arizona, 1967.

"Aventura en lo gris: Dos actos grises, unidos por un sueño
  increíble." *Teatro*. x (1954), 57-76.

BENÍTEZ CLAROS, RAFAEL. "Buero Vallejo y la condición hu-
  mana." *Visión de la literatura española*. Madrid, 1963.
  pp. 275-92.

BLAJOT, JORGE. "Del mundo mental de Buero Vallejo." *Reseña*.
  i (1964), 85-95.

BOREL, JEAN PAUL. "Buero Vallejo: Teatro y Política." *Revista
  de Occidente*. vi (Madrid, August, 1964), 226-234.

BOREL, JEAN PAUL. *El teatro de lo imposible.* Madrid: Guadarrama, 1966.

————. "Teatro de lo imposible." *Insula,* xvi, clxxix, 15.

————. *Théâtre de l'imposible.* (Neuchâtel), A la Baconnière.
Diff.: S.F.L., 1963.

BUERO VALLEJO, ANTONIO. "A propósito de 'Aventura en lo
gris.'" *Teatro.* ix (1963), 37-39, 78.

————. "A propósito de Brecht." *Insula,* xviii, cc (July-Aug.,
1963), 1, 14.

————. "Eurídice: 'Pieza negra.'" *Teatro.* ii (1954), 34-35.

————. *Gustavo Doré: Estudio crítico-biográfico.* Madrid: Cas-
tilla, 1949.

————. "La ceguera en mi teatro," *La carreta,* xii (Barcelona,
Sept., 1963), 5ff.

————. "Lo trágico." *Informaciones.* April 12, 1952.

————. "Me llamo Antonio Buero Vallejo." Discos Aguilar:
Madrid, 1964.

————. "Obligada precisión acerca del imposibilismo." *Primer
Acto.* xv (1960), 1-6.

————. "Sobre la tragedia," *Entretiens sur les Lettres et les
Arts,* xxii (Rodez, France, 1963), 57.

————. "Tragedia." *El teatro: Enciclopedia del arte escénico.*
Guillermo Díaz-Plaja, ed. Barcelona: Editorial Noguer, S. A.,
1958.

————. "Tres sonetos a la lluvia." *Grímpola.* v (1961).

————. "Tres sonetos en la lluvia." *Poesía Española.* i (1952),
21.

————. "Un poema y un recuerdo de Miguel Hernández."
Insula. clxviii (1960), 1, 17.

————. "Velázquez." *Grímpola.* v (1961).

CHANTRAINE, JACQUELINE VAN PRAAG. "Tendencias del teatro
español de hoy: Antonio Buero Vallejo y 'el buerismo.'"
Cuadernos Americanos. xxii, cxxx (Sept.-Oct., 1963), 254-263.

CELAYA, GABRIEL. "A Antonio Buero Vallejo." *Agora.* xli-xlii
(1960), 3.

CLEMENTELLI, ELENA. "Il teatro di Antonio Buero Vallejo."
Nuova Antologia. lxxxix (Roma, 1954), 140-42.

CLOCCHIATTI, EMILIO. "España y su teatro contemporáneo." *Cuadernos Hispanoamericanos*. lx (Madrid, 1964), 291-97.

"El conceptismo de Velázquez." *Insula*. clxii, 4.

CÓRDOBA, SANTIAGO. "Polémica entre el humor y el drama: Buero Vallejo y López Rubio, frente a frente." *Giornale di Metafisica*. vi (Génova, 1955), 50-51.

CORTINA, JOSÉ R. "El arte dramático de Antonio Buero Vallejo." Ph.D. thesis, University of Illinois, 1967.

DEVOTO, JUAN BAUTISTA. *Antonio Buero Vallejo: Un dramaturgo del moderno teatro español*. Eva Perón Tall. Gráf., de Menorca, 1954.

———. "La vivencia dramática de Buero Vallejo." *Teatro*. x (1954), 55-56.

DÍAZ-PLAJA, GUILLERMO. "Sobre 'La tejedora de sueños' de Buero Vallejo." *La voz iluminada*. Madrid, 1952, pp. 273-276.

———. "Theater in Spain (1960-61): The Artist Velázquez in the Theater." *Modern Drama*. iv, 179-83.

DÍEZ CRESPO, M. "Crítica del estreno de 'Irene, o el tesoro' de Buero Vallejo." *Giornale di Metafisica*. xxxvi (Génova, 1954), 63.

———. " 'El concierto de San Ovidio' en el Goya." *Arbor*. liii (Madrid, 1962), 475-76.

DOMENECH, RICARDO. "Inciso sobre el teatro." *Insula*. xvi, clxx, 4. (on Buero and "Las Meninas.")

———. "Notas sobre teatro: Crítica de 'Las Meninas.' " *Cuadernos Hispano-americanos*. xlii (Madrid), 119-24.

Don Juan y el teatro en España. Juan Gyenes, ed. Madrid: Ediciones Mundo Hispánico, 1957.

FERNÁNDEZ CUENCA, CARLOS. "Crítica del estreno de 'Casi un cuento de hadas' de Buero.' " *Teatro*. iv (1953), 4-7.

———. "Crítica de 'Madrugada.' " *Teatro*. x (1954), 6.

———. "En sólo una semana escribió Buero Vallejo la primera versión de 'En la ardiente oscuridad.' " *Correo Literario*. iv, lxix (Madrid, 1953), 12-15.

FERNÁNDEZ-SANTOS, ÁNGEL. "Antonio Buero Vallejo: 'El Concierto de San Ovidio.' " *Índice*. xvi, clxviii, 21.

———. " 'Las Meninas' de Antonio Buero Vallejo." *Índice*. xii, cxlv, 27-28.

FOSTER, DAVID WILLIAM. " 'Historia de una escalera': A Tragedy of Aboulia." *Renascence.* xvii (Fall, 1964), 3-10.

FRAILE, MEDARDO. "Twenty Years of Theater in Spain." trans. Mildred Boyer. *The Texas Quarterly: Image of Spain.* Austin: University of Texas, 1961.

GALINDO HERRERO, SANTIAGO. "Antonio Buero Vallejo: 'Las cartas boca abajo.' " *La Estafeta Literaria.* civ (Madrid, 1957), 10.

GARCIASOL, RAMÓN DE. "Sobre 'La tejedora de sueños.' " *Insula.* lxxiv (Feb., 1952).

HALSEY, MARTHA TALIAFERRO. "Buero Vallejo and the Significance of Hope." *Hispania.* li, i (Mar., 1968), 57-66.

――――. "The Tragedies of Antonio Buero Vallejo." *Dissertation Abstracts.* xxv (Ohio State University, 1964), 5278-79.

HOYO, ARTURO DE. "Sobre 'Historia de una escalera.' " *Insula.* xlvii (Nov., 1950).

Índice de Artes y Letras. l (Apr. 15, 1952). Includes an interview with Buero Vallejo about "Historia de una escalera."

J. M. S. "Teatro, verdad y poesía." *Papeles de Som Armadáns.* iii (Palma de Mallorca, 1956), 228-30. on "Hoy es fiesta."

LEFEBVRE, ALFREDO. "Algunas noticias de un dramaturgo español." *Atenea.* ccclxxv (Concepción, Chile, 1957), 52-57.

LÓPEZ GRADOLI, ALFONSO. "Notas sobre Buero Vallejo." *Gallo.* iv (1955), 6.

MAGAÑA SCHEVILL, ISABEL. "Lo trágico en el teatro de Buero Vallejo.» *Hispano.* vii, 51-58.

MANCINI GIANCARLO, GUIDO. "Figure del teatro spagnolo contemporaneo." *Quaderni di critica e storia della letteratura.* Luca (Edizioni Gruppo Culturale "Serra"), 1950.

MANZANARES DE CIRRE, M. "El realismo social de Buero Vallejo." *Revista hispánica moderna.* xxvii (1961), 320-324.

MARÍA Y CAMPOS, ARMANDO DE. " 'Historia de una escalera' de Antonio Buero Vallejo." *El teatro está siempre en crisis.* Méjico: Arriba el telón, 1944. pp. 133-43.

MARRA-LÓPEZ, JOSÉ R. "Conversación con Antonio Buero Vallejo." *Cuadernos del congreso por la libertad de la cultura.* xxxxii, 55-58.

MENOR, DAVID. "Casi un cuento de hadas." *Ateneo.* xxvi (1953), 22.

MONTERO, JOSÉ. "Una baraja en tres posturas." *La Estafeta Literaria.* cv (1957), 9-10.

NICHOLAS, ROBERT LEON. "The Evolution of Technique in the Theater of Antonio Buero Vallejo." Ph. D. thesis, University of Oregon, 1967.

NOBLE, BETH W. "Sound in the Plays of Buero Vallejo." *Hispania.* xli, 56-59.

PÉREZ MINIK, DOMINGO. "Buero Vallejo o la restauración de la máscara." *Teatro europeo contemporáneo.* Madrid, 1961, pp. 381-96.

QUINTO, JOSÉ MARÍA DE. "Crónica de teatro." *Insula.* ccxx (March, 1963), 19.

R. N. "Antonio Buero Vallejo, Premio March." *Mundo Hispánico.* cxxxxiv (1960), 34.

RODRÍGUEZ-CASTELLANO, JUAN. "Un nuevo comediógrafo español: Antonio Buero Vallejo." *Hispania.* xxxvii (March, 1954), 17-25.

ROIG, ROSENDO. "Talante trágico del teatro de Buero Vallejo." *Razón y fe.* clvi (1957), 363-367.

SALVAT, RICARD. *El teatre contemporani.* Barcelona, 1966. vol. 2, pp. 227-231.

SCHANZER, GEORGE C. "Remarks on the Theatrical Season in Madrid." *Hispania* xlvii (May, 1964), 337-39.

SHELNUTT, WILLIAM L. "Symbolism in Buero's 'Historia de una escalera.'" *Hispania.* xlii (March, 1959), 61-65.

SOLANO, FRANCISCO DE P. "O teatro de Buero Vallejo." *Rumo.* (1959), 343-55.

SORDO, ENRIQUE. "Buero Vallejo y 'Madrugada.'" *Revista.* Barcelona. iii, xcii (1954), 4.

Teatro Español. Madrid: Aguilar, S. A. Those volumes which contain Buero's plays also contain reviews. See the listing of his works.

TORRENTE BALLESTER, GONZALO. *Teatro español contemporáneo.* Madrid: Ediciones Guadarrama, S. L., 1957.

"Tres preguntas a Buero Vallejo." *Insula.* cxxxxvii (Feb., 1959), 4.

"Una encuesta sobre teatro." *Espectáculo.* Madrid, April, 1952.

VALBUENA PRAT, ÁNGEL. *Historia del teatro español*. Barcelona: Editorial Noguer, S. A., 1956.

VÁZQUEZ ZAMORA, RAFAEL. "La actualidad teatral." *Ínsula*. cxxxiv (Jan., 1958), 12.

―――. " 'Las cartas boca abajo' de Buero Vallejo." *Ínsula*. cxxxiv (1958), 15.

―――. "La señal que se espera." *Ínsula*. lxxviii (June, 1952).

―――. " 'Las Meninas' de Buero Vallejo en el Español." *Ínsula*. xvi, clxx, 15.

―――. "En el Goya, los trágicos ciegos de Buero Vallejo: en 'El Concierto de San Ovidio.' " *Ínsula*. xvii, cxciii (Dec., 1962), 16.

―――. " 'Un Soñador para un pueblo' de Buero Vallejo." *Ínsula*. xiv, cxlvii, 12.

VELÁZQUEZ, FLAVIA PAZ. "Forum a 'Las Meninas' de Buero Vallejo." *Revista de la Institución Teresiana*. xlix (1961), 8-9.

VIAN, FRANCISCO. "Il teatro di Buero Vallejo." *Vita e pensiero*. (Milán, marzo, 1952), 165-69.

CONTENTS

191

TORRES LIBRARY OF LITERARY STUDIES

1. RIPOLL, CARLOS: *Escritos desconocidos de José Martí.* Cuba, Puerto Rico. Propaganda revolucionaria. Juicios. Crítica. Estados Unidos.
2. GUILLERMO, EDENIA, AND JUANA AMELIA HERNÁNDEZ: *La novelística española de los 60:* Luis Martín Santos, Juan Marsé, Miguel Delibes, Juan Goytisolo, Juan Benet y Ana María Matute.
3. OJEDA, ENRIQUE: *Jorge Carrera Andrade. Introducción a su vida y obra.*
4. BELLINI, GIUSEPPE: *Quevedo en la poesía hispanoamericana del siglo XX: César Vallejo, Jorge Carrera Andrade, Octavio Paz, Pablo Neruda y Jorge Luis Borges.*
5. BALSEIRO, JOSÉ: *Novelistas españoles modernos.* 8th edition. Revised and enlarged.
6. RUPLE, JOELYN: *Antonio Buero Vallejo.* The First Fifteen Years.
7. LEON HILL, E.: *Miguel Ángel Asturias, lo ancestral en su obra literaria.*
8. GONZÁLEZ DEL VALLE, LUIS AND VICENTE CABRERA: *La nueva ficción hispanoamericana a través de Miguel Ángel Asturias and G. García Márquez.*
9. RIPOLL, CARLOS: *Índice Universal de la obra de José Martí.*
10. RIPOLL, CARLOS: *Archivo José Martí. Repertorio Crítico. Medio Siglo de Estudios Martianos.*
11. RIPOLL, CARLOS: *Patria: El Periódico de José Martí.* Registro General.
12. ORTEGA, JOSÉ: *Juan Goytisolo.* Alienación y agresión en Señas de Identidad y Reivindicación del conde Don Julián.
13. ORTEGA, JOSÉ AND FRANCISCO CARENAS: *Narradores españoles de la Guerra Civil.* Antología crítica.
14. URBANSKI, EDMUND S.: *Hispanoamérica y sus razas y costumbres.*
15. CASTILLO-PUCHE, J. L.: *Pío Baroja.*

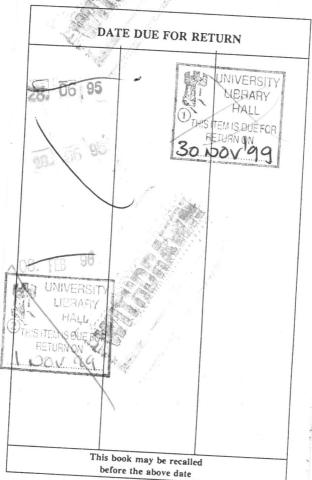